DEATH PAYS A DIVIDEND

SCRAP-IRON FOR JAPAN

The *Mogul Maru*, a Japanese freighter, waiting at Long Beach, California, for a load of No. 2 Heavy Melting Steel Scrap. *(Reproduced from "Life," April 19, 1937.)*

DEATH PAYS A DIVIDEND

by

FENNER BROCKWAY

and

FREDERIC MULLALLY

LONDON
VICTOR GOLLANCZ LTD
1944

CONTENTS

ACKNOWLEDGMENT

The authors wish to record their appreciation of the help given them by Miss Dorothy Detzer, Miss Dorothy Woodman, and Mr. Edward Owen Marsh in the preparation and presentation of the material used.

Some of the material used in the early chapters of this book is taken from *Bloody Traffic*, written by one of the present authors in 1933 and long since out of print.

CHAPTER I
CONSPIRATORS AGAINST PEACE

In a south-western suburb of London there is a woman who lost her only son in the World War of 1914–18. She must have loved that boy dearly, for when the news of his death was brought to her something broke and she became insane. More than a quarter of a century separates the rest of us from that war, but for this woman the clock stopped on a grey November morning of 1917.

She is still alive—a harmless lunatic. You can see her every morning fidgeting at the gate of her little bungalow, her straggly head bared to sun and rain. Unwary passers-by are called to the gate and told, in tones of breathless excitement, of a telegram she received "yesterday morning while I was wiping up the breakfast things"—a telegram from her boy, saying he was coming home on leave. "He should be here any moment now, any moment. Perhaps"—an eager, bright-eyed face is thrust up at you—"perhaps you passed him on the way along? A tall boy, wearing khaki, of course." You are sorry, you say gently, but you've not seen anyone answering to that description. Her smile fades as you pass on. A few seconds later it dances to life again as she strains over the gate to get a better glimpse of someone turning the corner into the road. In twenty-five years, this woman has not known a moment's real unhappiness: every waking moment is lively with the anticipation of joy.

But with her husband it is, of course, different. . . .

Not long after the outbreak of the second World War, one of the present writers was amazed to find him willing to discuss this war and the last without the slightest trace of bitterness or cynicism. Yes, he could remember the pledges that rang out over the waste and slaughter of 1914–18. The war to end all wars! A new era of permanent peace and world prosperity! He could remember, too, how quickly these pledges were forgotten at the peace conference and in the years that followed; opportunities that were squandered and frittered away by the agents of reaction,

nationalism and "sound" economy. He knows that his son,
and millions of other sons, died that those smooth pledges might
be redeemed. And now the world is joined in war again—*a war
which could have been prevented twenty-odd years ago*. Surely, he was
asked, surely those sons' and those parents' sacrifices were in
vain? "No," he replied, "not in vain. We won the war, didn't
we?"

There it is. *We won the war*. And now there is another one—
and we will win that. And provided there is no radical change
in the people's attitude, we will be at it again in ten, twenty
or thirty years' time and, of course, "we" will win that one
too! What a prospect for humanity—an unbroken succession
of military victories, each one more decisive than the last, more
far-reaching in its effects, more terrible in its toll of human life
and happiness!

Sooner or later the peoples will realize that the only victory
that matters is a victory over the things that make wars possible.
But before that day comes, the ordinary man and woman will
have to be able to distinguish between patriotism and nationalism;
race and racism; democracy and plutocracy, and a score of other
opposing values so cunningly reconciled and interwoven by the
demagogues and propagandists of capitalism and imperialism.
It may be that we shall not experience in our lifetimes such
an improvement in the general level of public enlightenment,
but we can at least hope that the major evils of the inter-war
years—the sins of omission that cry aloud for repentance—will
not escape the attention of a post-war world quickened and made
sensitive by its grim journey through this wasted time. *One of
these evils is the existence of an elaborately organized and financially
powerful vested interest devoted to the propagation of aggressive nationalism
and the multiplication of armaments.*

Let us be quite clear about one point. We do not suggest,
nor can any thoughtful person believe, that the international
armament groups have the power to *cause* wars. The farthest we
can go in this direction is to point out that they have made
technically possible certain minor wars (notably in South
America) plans for which might otherwise have been abandoned

at an earlier or later stage. What we do assert, however, and what this book sets out to establish as incontrovertible, is that it is impossible to achieve lasting peace throughout the world as long as there exists a powerful and influential grouping of forces which thrive on war and the preparation for war.

But it is here that the savage irony of the Marxist analysis of capitalistic development steps in. *The very organizational strength of the war industries is at the same time their greatest weakness.* A hundred years ago, the existence of independent armament manufacturers scattered widely throughout the "civilized" world might have been described, vaguely, as an "irritant" to aggression. Certainly no one would seriously have suggested that these unintegrated units had the power to jeopardize any thorough-going politico-economic formula for world peace. Today, however, they present a very different picture. On the national scene they appear as giant monopolistic combines dominating the vital steel and chemical industries and exerting, through the banks and their prodigious industrial investments, a powerful influence on the nation's financial and economic machinery. On the international scene they appear as giant octopodes with hundreds of tentacles—each one representing interlocking directorates or financial, trade and patents links. Collectively these powerful combines and cartels constitute, in the words of Admiral Lord Wester Wemyss, a vast "subterranean conspiracy against peace".[1] Their shares, as we shall see later, are held

---

[1] From an official memorandum laid before the Admiralty in 1918 by Lord Wemyss, at that time First Sea Lord. The phrase was used in the following passage, quoted by P. J. Noel Baker in Section 10 of the Minutes of Evidence taken before the Royal Commission on the Private Manufacture of and Trading in Arms:—

"Apart from the moral objections to the present system, which makes warfare a direct occasion of private gain, the system is attended by the inevitable consequence that the multiplication of armaments is stimulated artificially. Every firm engaged in the production of armaments and munitions of every kind naturally wants the largest possible output. Not only, therefore, has it a direct interest in the inflation of the Navy and Army Estimates and in war scares, but it is equally to its interest to push its foreign business. For the more armaments are increased abroad, the *more* they *must* be increased at home. This interrelation between foreign and home trade in armaments is one of the most subtle and dangerous features of the present system of private production. The evil is intensified by the existence

A 2

by leading statesmen and newspaper companies. They have built up through the years a frankenstein monster whose baleful activities will, when the public conscience is sufficiently aroused, bring about their final collapse from power. Their weakness lies in the remarkable degree of rationalization and centralization which characterizes their productive and distributive organisms —factors which render ultimate State expropriation a comparatively simple and immensely attractive operation.

It would be quite impossible in this book to do full analytical justice to the peculiarities of the armament industries' structure and the many technical aspects of private arms production. We would refer any reader interested in these subjects and in the broader field of cartel politics to the two standard works indispensable to any serious student—P. J. Noel Baker's *The Private Manufacture of Armaments* and Lenin's *Imperialism, The Highest Stage of Capitalism.*

This book is primarily concerned with the grave objections to a system of capitalist enterprise under which a powerful minority are able to derive profits and other material benefits from the misery and death of millions of their fellow-beings. Summarily, the case against private trading in arms is embodied in the following syllogism :—

(a) Private trading in arms has this in common with all other forms of modern capitalistic enterprise: it calls for the aggressive exploitation of actual and potential orders; the elimination, wherever possible, of trade competition, and the division of world markets between the leading groups and combines. These aims are most efficiently and profitably achieved by full collaboration on an international scale.

(b) Arms manufacturers are in business with one object and one object only—to derive the greatest amount of profit from the maximum sale of death-dealing instruments. In a world which has finally abandoned aggression as an instrument of

of international armament rings, the members of which notoriously play into each other's hands. So long as this subterranean conspiracy against peace is allowed to continue, the possibility of any serious concerted reduction of armaments will be remote."

foreign policy, the arms makers would go out of business: in a world at war, they prosper.

(c) Arms manufacturers are thus irresistibly impelled to favour the greatest degree of war mobilization and to view with positive hostility any attempt at partial or complete disarmament—*even when the political, economic and moral "irritants" are removed.* The practices adopted to overcome "sales resistance" range from the financing of "patriotic" defence leagues to the deliberate aggravation of international animosities.

Lest the concluding proposition be deemed excessively harsh and extravagant, we would draw the reader's attention to an official League of Nation's Report which reads, in part, as follows:—

"In general, the objections that are raised to untrammelled private manufacture may be grouped under the following headings:—

"1. That armament firms have been active in fomenting war scares and in persuading their own countries to adopt warlike policies and to increase their armaments.

"2. That armament firms have attempted to bribe Government officials, both at home and abroad.

"3. That armament firms have disseminated false reports concerning the military and naval programmes of various countries, in order to stimulate armament expenditure.

"4. That armament firms have sought to influence public opinion through the control of newspapers in their own and foreign countries.

"5. That armament firms have organized international armament rings through which the armament race has been accentuated by playing off one country against another.

"6. That armament firms have organized international armament trusts which have increased the price of armaments sold to governments." [1]

[1] From a report of the First Sub-Committee of the Temporary Mixed Commission established by the League in 1921.
Article 8, paragraph 5 of the League Covenant drew the attention of Members

In a House of Commons debate on November 8, 1934, Sir John Simon tried to convince his fellow Members that these six points merely represented *accusations* levelled against the armament interests: they were not intended to represent an established case against untrammelled private manufacture. The chapters which follow constitute an adequate answer to this and all other attempts by Government spokesmen to whitewash the Merchants of Death. They contain conclusive evidence of the validity of every single one of these charges.

---

to the "grave objections" to which private manufacture is open and states that "the Council shall advise how the evil effects attendant on such manufacture can be prevented".

CHAPTER II

STEEL HAS NO FATHERLAND

IT WOULD be of some interest, from the purely academic point of view, to be able to trace the historical development of the trade in armaments back to its earliest beginnings. We would find, perhaps, that even among the first men who ranged the European steppes some 40,000 years ago there was at least one bright fellow who found in spear-making a more profitable, and far less arduous, occupation than the tracking down of mammoths, sabre-toothed tigers and tribal enemies. Certain it is that from the first association of men in social groups and communities an increasingly important rôle has been played by those peculiar elements in every community who thrive on violence and grow fat on the agony of their fellow-beings.

Arms traders, like the poor, have always been with us; and it is a testimony to their resilience—or, if you prefer it, to man's incapacity for peace—that centuries of public opprobrium have done little, if anything, to check their activities or to eliminate the evils that follow inevitably from their existence.

Most of us are familiar with that allegorical concept of war— "The Four Horsemen of the Apocalypse"—engraved in 1494 by Albrecht Dürer and derived from the Book of Revelations (vi, 2–8). Dürer's masterpiece depicts four impetuous riders, Conquest, War, Death and the Profiteer, careering forward with supreme detachment over the writhing bodies of their less importunate contemporaries. The profiteer on his black horse (. . . "And I saw and behold a black horse; and he that sat thereon had a balance in his hand . . .") is given pride of place in the composition; and his features and general bearing have a quality of timelessness and immutability shared only by his right-hand man—Death. Trim his hair, exchange the extravagant garb of the period for the black coat and wing collar of today, put a large block of Ordinary shares in the hand swinging the balance, and you are left with a character-drawing of an aggressive, hard-faced capitalist that would not look out of place in any modern political cartoon.

The physical characteristics of the Merchants of Death have changed very little through the centuries—as the photographs of the leading figures in this country and in America will confirm. But their operational methods *have* undergone a profound change in the last hundred years, and it is this factor that renders a study of their early history of little practical value to the modern student.

It was not until the tail end of the nineteenth century that trading in arms could be said to have developed to a stage where it represented a positive menace to the cause of world peace. Up to that time, one owed one's first allegiance, in peace and in war, to one's own Government (the principal dispenser of arms orders) while waging a fierce and unremitting struggle against foreign competitors in the domestic and international markets.[1] With the emergence of monopoly-capitalism and the cartel system, the emphasis underwent a radical change. One's former enemies became one's best friends; differences were reconciled; competition gave way to collaboration; Englishman and German, German and Frenchman, Frenchman and American, all the leading capitalists of every industrial nation, sat down together and worked out their schemes for carving up the world to their mutual advantage and satisfaction.

[1] There were, of course, the usual exceptions to the general rule—notably the case of the Prussian gunmaker Alfred Krupp, who sold heavy artillery to his own Government *and* the Austrian Government for use in the Prussian-Austrian War of 1866. "At the famous battle of Königgratz," writes Dr. Lehmann-Russbüldt (*War for Profits*, p. 42), "German soldiers, bound by blood ties, destroyed each other with German guns which were molten, brotherly-wise, in the same crucible; and likewise in brotherly fashion the profits flowed into the self-same coffers." Later, Krupp tried—without success—to sell his wares to Napoleon III for use in the Franco-Prussian War of 1870. In a letter addressed to the French Emperor on April 29, 1868, he stressed the fact that he had already supplied steel cannon to "several powerful European Governments" (he himself underlined these words). The reply of the Emperor, sent by General le Boeuf, read as follows :—

"The Emperor has received your prospectus with great interest, and His Majesty commands that his thanks be conveyed to you for this. I am requested to inform you that His Majesty extends his lively wishes for the success and expansion of an industry which promises to be of considerable service to mankind."

The usual form of arrangement was the exchange of licences involving rights to manufacture (on a royalty basis) certain types of weapon for sale in certain parts of the world. Supplemented by price-fixing agreements and profit-sharing schemes, these arrangements had the effect of partitioning the world into cosy, water-tight sales areas over which the armament cartels were able to wield a virtually unchallenged bargaining-power. The real danger in this new development lay not so much in the mitigation of economic rivalry as in the fact that the various cartel partners' hitherto strongly entrenched sense of patriotism (perhaps "nationalism" is the better word) became, for the first time, a thing apart from—and, in certain circumstances, a positive obstacle to—the advancement of their own personal interests. To them, the only potential enemy was the "barren theorist" of disarmament: a foreign Government which placed lucrative armament orders with one's own firm or one's licencee became, automatically, a "friend".

Thus, you had the situation—repeated over and over again since the turn of the last century—where Country A has equipped itself militarily to attack Country B by the large-scale purchase of armaments and inventions from the nationals of the enemy State.

The armament cartels were well established many years before the outbreak of the first World War. They sensed, only too clearly, the rapid deterioration in international confidence which preceded that disaster and, untroubled by any narrow considerations of patriotism and world peace, they set out to exploit the situation to the full—to derive the maximum amount of benefit from the feverish, beat-your-neighbour armaments scramble which swept Europe.

This chapter is devoted to a review of some of their activities prior to and during the war of 1914–18. This may appear to be ancient history to some of our readers; but it will bear repetition just as long as the Merchants of Death remain in a position to retrace their steps when the present, war-time restrictions are removed.

Preparing the Stage

First, let us dispose of any doubts as to the accuracy of the statement made above: that the armament cartels and combines were fully aware of the tension that existed in Europe before the first World War and, in the natural line of their business, set out to aggravate that tension by indiscriminate sales both to the potential aggressors and the potential victims of aggression. We take an example from America. The following statement occurs in the text of a representation made to the U.S. Bureau of Internal Revenue, after the last war, by the attorney for Colt's Patent Firearms Manufacturing Co., which enjoyed a virtual monopoly over certain types of small arms and machine-guns:—

"We appreciate the extraordinary demand occasioned by the World War. We knew that a tremendous conflict was brewing in Europe; we felt this in 1908 and spent the money necessary to organize and maintain a sales force all over Europe."

In connection with the same tax case, the company's President, Mr. Samuel M. Stone, recorded the following information:—

"In 1908, I went to Europe as a representative of the Colt's Patent Firearms Manufacturing Co. The trip to Europe was largely influenced by enquiries the company was receiving from agents or representatives for various Governments, which indicated a keen, active interest in the subject of firearms of all kinds by many of the European nations. It was our desire to ascertain to what extent we would be capable of satisfying demands which apparently were likely to be made upon us. . . .

"I went to Turkey at the invitation of representatives of that Government, and they purchased small arms through our agents [*later used against British and Australian troops at Gallipoli*] [1] commencing their purchases about 1909. . . . We maintained an office in London, England, which kept in touch with the British Empire, also at Hamburg, Germany. . . . From 1908, our sales to foreign Governments steadily increased, and I

[1] Italicised interpolations in brackets are the author's.

knew that there was then a market which could be greatly expanded in the immediate future.[1]

"Indications were that Europe at that time was preparing for a war. Great secrecy was imposed upon all military observers, attachés and foreign embassies. I had personal knowledge of the desire on the part of the Italian Government to build a Government armoury for the manufacture of small arms in 1908, and everything in Europe pointed to an increasing demand for arms similar to the ones covered by patents owned by this company. I visited Vienna, Austria, in December, 1908, and this Government was then seeking automatic pistols and machine guns. . . ."

The market price of Colt's stock rose from 79½ in 1908 to 182 in 1913, and net earnings over the same period rose from $251,451 to $653,659. In order to take full advantage of the pre-war scramble for armaments, the company was forced, from 1908 onwards, to earmark a large proportion of its current profits and *anticipated* earnings for the expansion of plant capacity. The return of this capital expenditure was entirely dependent on the continuation of the arms race and the ultimate outbreak of war.

"The situation would have been desperate for Colt if its thorough preparations for war had not been followed by war." [2]

[1] When war is brewing, the most effective way of "expanding markets" is to follow the course—so ably pursued by Mr. Stone in Europe—of letting a Government know that its potential enemy in the impending conflict is in possession of a particular type of weapon. Fear of military inferiority does the rest, and a counter-balancing order invariably follows for the same type of weapon. That the playing off of one country against another was the recognised practice of the Colt company is confirmed in a letter addressed to the company by its agent in Latin America on September 22, 1923. The letter, from which the following sentence is extracted, was exhibited during the Nye Committee's hearings in February, 1936. The names of the Governments concerned were omitted to avoid repercussions in South America :—

". . . If the X Government buy (our guns) it will be a larger order than (certain other countries) put together; and if they decide on Colt, that will be a strong inducement for the others to do the same."

[2] Nye Committee Report No. 944, Part 3, p. 39.

During this period when, as Mr. Stone has stated elsewhere, "every intelligent person knew that a titanic struggle was bound to come very soon" and that Britain and Germany would certainly not be allies in this struggle, we find the British, German and American partners in the chemicals' cartel operating under an agreement for the exchange of military inventions and the sharing of profits. In 1907, a contract was signed between du Pont Powder Co., as one party, and Vereinigte Koln-Rottweiler Pulverfabriken and Nobel Dynamite Trust (predecessor of Imperial Chemical Industries), jointly, as the other party, under which each party was required to disclose "full particulars in regard to all inventions employed by such party", and "to appoint one or more trustworthy persons experienced in the business for the purpose of receiving information from the other party as to all secret processes now used by either party", and to disclose to such appointees of the other party all "such information concerning any secret process used, owned, or controlled by such party". The party spirit seems to dance its way through this happy little agreement—*which remained operative up to January 1, 1913*, when a new secret-processes agreement was drafted, but prevented, by the outbreak of war, from coming into operation.

Having pooled their military secrets, it was only right and proper that these Men without Countries should do the same with the surplus profits accruing from this arrangement. To this end, the world was split up into three broad sections, or sales areas. The British and German combines received Europe, Africa and Asia; du Pont received the United States, most of Central America and Colombia and Venezuela, and in the remaining territory—Canada, Newfoundland, British Honduras, European possessions in the Caribbean, and the rest of South America—each side received non-exclusive rights in the inventions of the other. The British and German partners received 36½% of all du Pont operating profits in excess of 1906 profits, and du Pont received 63½% of the European companies' profits similarly computed.

In 1906, the world still had eight long years in which to avert the cataclysm of 1914. Common-sense, the subordination of imperialist pride and nationalist greed to the nobler interests of common humanity—above all, *the complete suppression of any influences making for international tension and suspicion*—might well have turned the balance so delicately poised throughout those fateful years. This view was endorsed, two years after the end of hostilities, by one of the greatest and best-informed English statesmen of those times—Mr. Lloyd George—when he said:—

"The more one reads memoirs and books, written in the various countries, of what happened before August 1, 1914, the more one realizes that no one at the head of affairs quite meant war at that stage. It was something into which they glided, or rather staggered and stumbled, perhaps through folly; and a discussion, I have no doubt, would have averted it."

But discussion, to be fruitful, must be conducted in an atmosphere of mutual confidence—a condition which, as we shall shortly see, was made impossible of achievement by the sinister activities of those who stood to gain everything by war and the large-scale preparation for war. In his book *Twenty-five Years*, Lord Grey, Foreign Secretary from 1905 to 1915, wrote: "The enormous growth of armaments in Europe; the sense of insecurity and fear caused by them—it was these that made war inevitable. This, it seems to me, is the truest reading of history."

How were the arms merchants able to stimulate this "enormous growth", this sense of insecurity and fear? Their methods were many and various; but easily the most successful and least expensive of them was the simple, time-dishonoured device—the War Scare.

The classic war scare of this century was first set in motion *in 1909* by Mr. H. H. Mulliner, then managing director of the Coventry Ordnance Co. The economic policy of the Liberal Government from 1908 onwards had dealt the armament firms a severe blow. From 1908 to 1910, the dividends of Vickers and Armstrong fell from 15% to 10%. The *Naval Annual* published at the beginning of 1909 recorded that "the shipbuilding industry has passed through one of the worst years ever known". Unless

Government orders could be increased there was every prospect of the dividend falling even farther. Orders for warships would not come unless a feeling of insecurity were created. A feeling of insecurity would not come without a war scare. The war scare was started.

On March 3, 1909, Mr. Mulliner convinced the Admiralty that he had private information of such importance that the Cabinet was justified in taking the unprecedented step of receiving him to hear his story. He told the Cabinet that he had reliable information that the German Government was secretly accelerating its naval programme. The Cabinet accepted his story, and Mr. Asquith and Mr. McKenna hurried to the House of Commons to announce that Germany would have seventeen Dreadnoughts by March, 1912, instead of the nine announced in her naval programme. Mr. Balfour, who had also been admitted into Mr. Mulliner's confidence, went farther. He declared that Germany would have twenty-five, or at the lowest estimate twenty-one, Dreadnoughts by that date. The House became panic-stricken. It immediately voted an increase of naval expenditure of £4,603,002—of which £4,409,502 went to the private armament firms. But even this was not regarded as enough. The war scare, once started, was fanned to flame by the nationalist and "patriotic" Press and by politicians who demanded still more Dreadnoughts. The Tories won a by-election at Peckham by a sensational majority on the cry "We Want Eight and We Won't Wait!" Before the end of the year, the Government responded to the popular clamour and ordered four more Dreadnoughts.

The effect which this single scare had on the whole issue of war and peace can be judged from the following facts. Mr. Churchill proposed a naval holiday to Germany, and he afterwards declared (*The Times*, November 15, 1933): "I laboured for peace before the war, and if the naval holiday I advised had been accepted by Germany, *the course of history might have been different*". The Germans, however, rejected the proposed naval holiday on the advice of Admiral von Tirpitz, the leader of the powerful Navy Party, who convinced the Government that the proposal was only another dishonest British manœuvre "like the

Mulliner scare". Von Tirpitz thus succeeded in getting through his supplementary Naval Bill of 1912, although the Chancellor, Bethmann-Hollweg, feared that this bill "would lead to war with England". The attempt to restore Anglo-German confidence was thus wrecked. In his book *Before the War*, Lord Haldane wrote:—

"Discussion about the terms of a formula became rather futile and we had only one course left open to us: to respond by quietly increasing our navy and concentrating its strength in the northern seas. This was done with great energy by Mr. Churchill, the result being that as the result of the administration of the Fleet by Mr. McKenna and himself, the estimates were raised by over 20 millions to 51 millions."

When March, 1912, came, the Mulliner story proved to be completely without justification. As Mr. Churchill says in his book *World Crisis* (page 37):—

"The gloomy Admiralty anticipations were in no respect fulfilled in the year 1912. The British margin was found to be ample in that year. *There were no secret German Dreadnoughts, nor had Admiral von Tirpitz made any unproved statement in respect of major construction.*"

But the object of the scare had been achieved. Large contracts were handed out to British armament firms, naval rivalries were revived and the first World War made inevitable. The dividends of Vickers and Armstrong shot up again. "I find, in the year before the scare, Messrs. Vickers' profits amounting to £424,000," said Mr. Philip Snowden in the House of Commons on March 17, 1914. "Two years after that they were nearly double the amount. Every year since the success of the intrigue their profits have gone up—£474,000; £544,000; £745,000; £872,000." Mr. Mulliner, however, deserves some sympathy, for he was treated most ungenerously by the Government. Coventry Ordnance Co. received none of the orders which he was so instrumental in inspiring, although its parent firm, Cammell Laird, got one of the first contracts. It was Mr. Mulliner's righteous indignation against the Government that led him to give away the secret of the scare. Shortly afterwards he was pensioned off from the management of his company.

HANDS ACROSS THE BATTLE-FRONTS

Well, they got their war—these Men without Countries. And it was a war such as armament manufacturers the world over had conceived only in their wildest dreams. Profits flowed into their coffers in a seemingly endless torrent—while tragedy, death and suffering stalked the battlefield and the home. There were times, in those four ghastly years, when it seemed that the cup of human suffering could hold no more, that the common people would revolt against the frightful, ever-mounting toll of lives out in those European wastelands. Then the Merchants of Death would suddenly realize that they *had* countries, after all; and they would take time off from their board-meetings to address the workers and the wives and mothers of the fighting-men. They would lecture them on the virtues of patriotism, the glory of dying for one's dear Fatherland or Motherland. "Rule Britannia!"; "Vive La France!"; "Deutschland über Alles!"—everywhere it was the same. Then.

But it had been quite different before the war; and it was to be quite different again afterwards. Study, for example, the principal clauses in an agreement (mentioned in the Reichstag in 1913) between Belgian, Austrian and German firms:—

"The traffic of arms, respecting the deliveries of remodelled machine-guns or carbine rifles for Russia, Japan, China and Abyssinia, will be carried on for mutual benefit, and the estimated earnings will be distributed to the various groups according to a predetermined scale. The two groups of factories will give each other as much mutual help as possible, in order that every factory may be able to manufacture the required arms in the cheapest and quickest manner.

"To this end, figures and dimension tables of the desired model under production, the required measuring instruments and calibres, shall be handed over at their respective cost price, in so far as possible, or lent *gratis*. The price of the arms to be delivered is to be at all times determined mutually by the groups.

"In order to carry out the fundamental views expressed earlier, a common chest will be established in which every factory which manufactures, markets or delivers rifles and carbines on its own initiative, shall be obliged to pay a fee of fifteen francs per weapon."

Patriotism seems to play a very minor rôle in this agreement, by which one country (Germany) not only supplied a future enemy (Russia) with rifles and machine-guns, but actually shared the resulting profits with another future enemy (Belgium)! The British manufacturers were not less active in the years leading up to the war. "Vickers", said Mr. Hugh Dalton in the House of Commons in 1926, "had been supplying [*just before the war*] the Turkish Artillery with shells which were fired into the Australian, New Zealand and British troops as they were scrambling up Anzac Cove and Cape Hellas. Did it matter to the directors of these armament firms, so long as they did business and expanded the defence expenditure of Turkey, that their weapons mashed up into bloody pulp all the morning glory that was the flower of Anzac—the youth of Australia and New Zealand and our own country?"[1]

In his evidence before the Royal Commission on the Private Manufacture of and Trading in Arms in May, 1935, Mr. S. F. Perry of the Co-operative Party made the following statement:—

"Some years ago I had the opportunity of speaking in the town of Bedford. In the interval before the meeting, I was walking around the town and saw one of the usual war trophies [*a gun captured from the enemy*]. On that trophy there is a brass plate with this inscription: 'Presented to the town of Bedford by the 5th Bedfordshire Regiment. Captured at Gaza.' As I

[1] As late as 1914, Armstrong Whitworth and Vickers jointly undertook the reorganization of the Turkish Navy and Turkish dockyards. (See Noel Baker's *The Private Manufacture of Armaments*, p. 72.)

read that plate, I pictured the deeds of heroism of the young boys of the Bedfordshire Regiment, and I knew too of some of the desolate homes in Bedford. Then I walked around to the other side of the gun, and on the other side of the gun there is an inscription in much larger letters. That inscription read: 'Made by Sir George Armstrong Whitworth & Co.'"

The case for the defence was put before the Royal Commission in October, 1935, by Admiral Sir Reginald Bacon, K.C.B., K.C.V.O., D.S.O., managing director of the Coventry Ordnance Works, 1910–15:—

"I have seen it stated", he said, "that British ammunition was used against our troops at Gallipoli. That is very likely. Why should it not be? I think at that particular moment the German ammunition was probably a little better than ours, but the main point is that if they had not used English ammunition they would have used German, which would have been to the disadvantage of our troops [not to mention "our" manufacturers]. The reason I say that the German ammunition was better than ours is that they had better fuses for their shells. They were the leading nation is fuse manufacture at that time."

On the face of it, this statement would appear logical enough. But the good Admiral overlooked one very important fact. *The patent rights on these superior German fuses were made available to Vickers, some time before the war, by Krupp; and Vickers were therefore able to offer the Turkish War Department a product in every respect the equal—and in some respects the superior—of that marketed by their German "competitor".* Krupp, of course, were entitled to a handsome royalty on all such sales, and it was often a matter of complete indifference to them whether foreign orders went to one of their licensees or to themselves. Thus, the only satisfaction left to the Allied soldiers at Gallipoli lay in the fact that the shells which tore, crippled and killed them were of the Best British Make. None of this shoddy, foreign stuff.

In this connection, it is interesting to recall that Krupp sued

Vickers, after the last war, for 1*s*. on every hand grenade containing the Krupp-patented fuse supplied to the British forces on the Western Front. The amount claimed was £6,150,000, which means that 123,000,000 fuses of the German type were used against the soldiers of Germany and her allies. A compromise was reached under which Krupp was given a large interest in the British-owned Miers Steel and Rolling Mills in Spain.

It is only too obvious that whoever else suffers from the indiscriminate traffic in arms, it is never the Merchants of Death or their loyal shareholders. A further instance of this was the device adopted, during the last war, to dissolve the German-British partnership in the International Cartel of Powder Manufacturers. Despite the proclamations which were issued for the confiscation of enemy property, the Nobel Dynamite Trust succeeded in obtaining passports for the British and German agents to meet to arrange for the exchange of shares. Advertisements were published in the Press of both countries in May, 1915, announcing an exchange of shares between the British and German sections of the Trust, and the announcement was introduced by the statement that it was made "with the consent of the two Governments". The shareholders were assured that the "Ordinary shares of the Nobel Dynamite Co. held in Germany will be accepted in exchange for the same class of shares in the Dynamite Aktien Gesellschaft (formerly the Alfred Nobel Co., of Hamburg)" and *vice versa*. By this means British shareholders in the German company, which was producing explosives to shatter British soldiers to bits, were protected against a loss of their interest and dividends.

Now let us turn to one further illustration of what Senator Nye meant when he said that "the only thing left to be honoured at all in time of war is a patent on war machines". Up to 1914, it was impossible for any Government to build electricity-driven submarines without a licence from the Electric Boat Co. of New York. In June, 1912, the necessary licence was granted to the Whitehead Co. of Trieste, Austria, which—on the outbreak of war—immediately handed over to the Germans all the vital

technical information it had derived from this agreement.[1]
Thousands of British and American non-combatants were sent
to a watery grave as a result of von Tirpitz's ruthless submarine
campaign—a campaign which constituted a flagrant breach of
international law. But the Electric Boat Co. was more concerned
with Germany's breach of international patent rights, and entered
a claim before the American-German Mixed Claims Commission for $40,000 on each of the 400 U-boats built to their
design (the ultimate recovery was only $125,000). Had they
known that Germany was to treat them so scurvily, the directors
of the Electric Boat Co. might not have refused, as they did, to
hand over to the U.S. Navy Department certain German patent
rights which they safeguarded throughout the war.[2]

It is commonly assumed that, immediately on the outbreak of
war, all cartel agreements between armament combines registered
in the belligerent countries are automatically rendered null and
void; that the Bloody International is dissolved and its former
partners ranged solidly behind their respective Governments.
This assumption is not necessarily correct. War, to the Men
without Countries, represents little more than a temporary
departure from the practice normally followed in the marketing
of their products. For the moment, the full capacity of their
factories is monopolized by a particular Government in the
interests of a particular nation; but they know only too well
that their very existence, in this age of shifting values and rapid
political change, depends on the preservation—if only in spirit—
of their international structure, and the waging of an integrated

---

[1] The agreement (dated June 11, 1912) was worded as follows:—

"The American Company hereby grants to the Whitehead Company
for the term of twenty years from the date hereof the exclusive right during
the continuance of this licence to manufacture submerged boats in Austria-
Hungary in accordance with the said patents, secrets and designs, or any
other letters patent now and hereafter belonging to the American Company
or which may either directly or indirectly come under its control relating to
or connected with submerged boats, all of which are hereinafter referred to
as 'the American Company's patents', and to sell the same exclusively in
Austria-Hungary, Greece, Turkey, Rumania and Bulgaria, for the use of the
respective Governments of those countries."

[2] Nye Committee Hearings, Part 1, p. 228.

rearguard action against any politico-economic measures which might jeopardize the post-war regrouping of their forces.

When one nation is locked in deadly conflict with another it is unlikely that a kindly view will be taken of any attempt at brotherly collaboration between its own armament manufacturers and those of the enemy State. For this very good reason, the conspirators are driven underground and forced to thrash out their mutual problems in the secrecy of board-rooms in their own and in neutral countries. On rare occasions a corner of the veil is lifted and the public given one brief glimpse of the conspirators at work, before the politicians and newspaper proprietors rush forward to block up the gap with their specious arguments and spurious apologetics.

One such instance, in the first World War, concerned a gentleman's agreement between the French and German industrialists of the Briey Basin. The full story was first publicized in this country by C. K. Streit in articles written for *Foreign Affairs*[1] in 1920. The following quotation is from an introduction to these articles by the late E. D. Morel:—

"His narrative is a revelation of staggering implications. He takes us by the hand to the mouth of the hell which capitalists and financiers prepare for the common people of the world. 'My country, right or wrong!' That is the parrot cry with which millions delude themselves when iron magnates, secret diplomats, armament manufacturers and the proprietors of newspaper trusts have succeeded in hounding nations into war; and they themselves, the pitiful sheep, fed for a season until their time has come to be devoured; encouraged to breed so that the supply of meat shall be maintained. But sheep just as long as they are prepared to remain sheep."

The Briery Basin, in Lorraine, was invaded by the Germans soon after the outbreak of war, and remained in their unchallenged possession until the end of the war. Not until the American offensive in the direction of Briey at the end of 1918 did the Allies threaten the possession of the district which, before the

[1] A Union of Democratic Control publication.

war, had produced 70% of France's iron ore. That the Briey ore was of vital importance to the German war machine was confirmed by the German Chancellor himself on May 20, 1915, when he declared that "if the production of minerals in Lorraine were disturbed, the war would be almost lost". It was not disturbed: the de Wendels saw to that.

The de Wendel family, together with the French Schneider-Creusot group, owned large properties on both sides of the frontier running through Lorraine. On the German side they owned concessions producing 3,000,000 tons of iron ore a year; on the French side they owned mines producing nearly 1,000,000 tons a year. Underground tunnels connected the two areas in which the properties were located. François de Wendel was President of the *Comité des Forges* (the equivalent of the British Iron and Steel Federation), Conservative member of the Chamber of Deputies for Meurthe-et-Moselle and part owner of the most prominent Nationalist newspaper, the *Journal des Débats*, and the popular *Le Temps*. The German Thyssen group controlled mines in the Briey Basin and, prior to the war, formed a special French company to operate during the war period.

"It is understood" (reported *Paris L'Œuvre* on May 22, 1917) "that a part of the profits realized by this company in the making of war munitions for France will be put aside for the Thyssen group, and that after the war, automatically and legally, Messrs. Thyssen will receive this large sum. As it is certain that those same Thyssens work also for the war in Germany, these interesting metallurgists receive their profits then with both hands—from furnishing material to Germany and to France. If money has no odour, steel has no fatherland."

Now here the story becomes really interesting. Rather belatedly, French politicians came to suspect that there was something sinister about the tranquility on the Lorraine front up to 1918, and shortly after the war an official committee of investigation was appointed to look into the whole matter. The following are extracts from the Chamber of Deputies debates which followed the publication of the committee's report:—

Deputy Barthe: "I have affirmed that, during the war, a general was officially reprimanded for having bombarded the district of Briey by airplanes and that, at that period of the war, the military chiefs forbade the aviators to bomb this basin. Among those who, not wishing to give in to such orders because they noticed the activity of the Germans in the Briey Basin, went and bombarded it, I believe some have been punished."

Deputy Flandin (a Conservative who had served at Verdun as an artillery officer): "During this difficult period (the latter part of 1916) we soldiers at the front often wondered why our aviation, which was so active during the battle of Verdun, had not been ordered to intervene and bombard the mines and smelters from which arose immense clouds of smoke which we saw on clear days covering the horizon in the direction of Conflans. And so, on December 23, 1916, I went to the headquarters of General Guillaumet commanding the Second Army, and explained the situation, giving him a detailed map of the Briey mines and smelters. A few days later, I and my comrades were overjoyed to see that a squadron of the Second Army had bombarded the de Wendel mines at Joeuf. But no other such bombardments followed. Puzzled, I returned to the Army's headquarters. There the chief of staff told me that the general had been ordered to cease these operations for two reasons— because Joeuf, it seemed, was not in the Second Army's sector and because the General Staff reserved to itself the right to give orders of this kind to the bombing squadrons." (Cynical laughter from the other deputies.)

Albert Thomas (Minister of Munitions): "At the end of 1916, during Briand's second ministry, whilst General Lyautey was Minister for War, I demanded the bombardment of Briey several times, and the Council of Ministers was annoyed at the inactivity of the Air Force. The War Minister announced that he had given the order for the bombardment of Briey several times but that his orders had not been executed. . . . The reason given by General Lyautey for the attitude of the General Staff was the insufficient number of planes and strength

. . . to which we replied (it was the moment of the repressive attacks) that if there were enough planes for open towns there were also enough for Briey."

Finally, after twenty-seven months of "phoney war", several bombing expeditions were sent over the area, but these were skilfully arranged to avoid doing any real damage. Deputy Eynac, describing the first bombing to the Chamber on February 14, 1919, said : "The orders of the objectives to bombard were given to the bombing group in execution of a bombing plan—a secret document established under the direction of Lieutenant Lejeune, at that time attached to the aviation section of the group of armies in the East. This plan received the approbation of the Grand General Staff. Frequently, in telephone messages or in visits to the bombing squadrons, Lieutenant Lejeune, who indicated the objectives of the day or for the moment, repeated the order *prohibiting the aviators from attacking certain objectives situated within the blockaded railroad lines.*"

One would have to be ingenuous to a degree not to suspect some connection between Lejeune's concern for certain Briey industries and the fact that he was, in peace-time, an employee of the *Comité des Forges*, of which de Wendel was President !

An echo of the Briey exposure came in April, 1936, when M. Boussotrot, then chairman of the French Aviation Committee, stated that during the first World War he had bombed the German-occupied works at Briey, *and that on his return he was court-martialled and punished.*

The war of 1914–18 was hailed as the "war to end all wars"; but it was far from being regarded as such by the Merchants of Death. No sooner had the firing died down on the Western Front than the armament manufacturers turned their attention towards new fields of "enterprise". Vickers and Schneider-Creusot, old friends and joint owners of the Vickers-Schneider Co., soon became aware that all was not going too well between Greece and Turkey. So Vickers decided that Greece was the champion of human rights, and armed that country (at a very good profit) for its attack on Turkey. The Turks, meanwhile, had found an unexpected but equally formidable "ally" in Schneider-Creusot, with whose help they were able to inflict a decisive military defeat on the Greeks outside Angora in September, 1922. The Greeks were driven out of Asia Minor and Thrace, and Smyrna was looted and thousands of her inhabitants massacred. The following thumb-nail impression by an American press correspondent is quoted by Professor Delaisi in *What Would Be the Character of Another War?*

"I first saw the retreat of the Greeks; they abandoned cannon and machine-guns all bearing the mark of the British firm of Vickers. Then I witnessed the triumphal entry of the Turks into Smyrna; they brought with them magnificent Creusot cannon. That day I understood the meaning of the *Entente Cordiale*."

CHAPTER III

GREMLINS AT GENEVA

IN THE First World War, 12,000,000 human beings were killed on the battlefields and 25,000,000 more sickened and died from the famine and pestilences which the conflict of man against man brings in its wake.

Among our readers there will be some who, even now in the height of the Second World War, can feel the dreadful reality of this statement; can react emotively to its meaning. But they are an isolated minority. The politicians tell us today—as they told our fathers and grandfathers before us—that we are "living in the presence of history". It is a noble phrase; round, solid—and curiously comforting. It means that we are living in the presence of wholesale butchery, stupendous waste and unending destruction. It means more: it means that we must take these things for granted, never doubting their necessity, never flagging in our killing, squandering and destroying until "victory" is won. Some there are, here and in the enemy countries, who refuse to fight for the kind of victory that a world war brings: they are branded, by us and our enemies, as traitors, cowards and "fifth-columnists". Others sublimate their inborn hatred of war in a new-found passion for "their" country, for the rights of oppressed minorities, for a democratic heritage which they have never yet enjoyed— save in an abstract, political sense. Others, and they are many, are swept joyously into war by surge of hatred against Nazi tyranny and outraged patriotism. To most of us, when the fighting finally ends and we are able to measure the gains against the losses, come disillusionment and a powerful reaction against war as an instrument for settling international grievances.

After the last war, this reaction expressed itself in world-wide sympathy with the concept of an international court of arbitration to which every nation would have to submit its grievances and by which any aggressor-State would be brought to account. World history from 1919 to 1939 is largely a record of the attempt, and failure, to realize this ideal of an organized peace through the instrumentality of the League of Nations. The present writers do not intend—nor would it be possible within the scope of this book—to attempt a detailed analysis of the causes which contributed to this failure. They believe that when the bone of contention has finally been picked dry, history will record the simple verdict that the League failed, not through any serious organizational weakness, but because it was committed, from the start, to the perpetuation of an inequitable division of world wealth among the member-States. But there was another development brought on by the reaction from the last war which, though strictly inseparable from the general problem of the League, does merit especial attention in this study.

With the cessation of hostilities, the nations of the world were faced with the formidable task of reconstruction and economic rehabilitation. The early accomplishment of this task demanded the maximum diversion of man-power and industrial capacity to normal, peace-time activity and the maximum degree of confidence and trust on the international political plane. This, in turn, depended on the success of the League's plans for partial world disarmament and the control of the international trade in arms, whose "evil effects" were formally recognized by all the signatories to the League Covenant. The ordinary people everywhere had decided that such a programme was both desirable and practicable; that efficient supervision by League commissions would ensure the strict observance of its provisions in every country which became a party to the proposed agreements. Let us now see how the arms manufacturers and traders conspired together to undermine this programme, to frustrate any effective legislation directed against the bloody traffic, to strangle at birth this great experiment in organized disarmament.

In 1924 the Assembly of the League of Nations directed the Secretary General to inform member- and non-member-States of a proposed Convention for the Control of the International Trade in Arms, Munitions and Implements of War, and to invite them to take part in a conference on the subject to be held at Geneva during the following year. The draft convention contained nothing that could be described as revolutionary, or even

B

controversial, by any nation seriously concerned with the evils of untrammelled trading. There was no attempt to abolish private manufacture or to *prohibit* trading between Governments and individuals throughout the world. The sole purpose of the convention was to introduce the principles of licensing, inspection and supervision; to shift the responsibility for any transactions calculated to stir up international strife from the slippery shoulders of the manufacturers to those of the Governments directly concerned. In short, the only people likely to suffer from the ratification of the proposed convention were those who, in the past, had profited most from the aggravation of international rivalries and who hoped to extend their activities into the future.

These elements sprang to action immediately. Another kind of international conference—this time of gunmakers—was arranged to take place in Paris on February 16 and 17, 1925, with the expressed purpose of planning the defeat of the draft convention which the responsible Governments of the world were to consider at the official Geneva conference to be held three months later.

The Gunmakers' Congress was organized by the Committee of the Liége Gunmakers' Association of Belgium, and there is considerable significance in the fact that one of the committee's first moves was to enlist the sympathy and active co-operation of the American armament interests. The American Government, whose refusal to join the League of Nations had dealt such a serious blow to the conception of collective security, had actually agreed to send delegates to this Geneva conference. It was strongly felt in League circles that if the U.S. delegates could be persuaded to endorse, and their Government to ratify, the draft convention, the way would be open to further U.S. participation in the League's activities.

The Liége Gunmakers, only too well aware that the situation had taken a dangerous turn, decided that the wisest course would be to get the American companies to "turn on the heat" in such a way that the U.S. delegates would leave for Geneva *under instructions to oppose the convention irrespective of the degree of support it obtained from other nations represented at the conference.*

Accordingly, on December 5, 1924, the Liége committee

addressed a letter to the Winchester Repeating Arms Co. drawing its attention to the terms of the draft convention—which, they took pains to stress, were "elaborated without taking information as to the opinion of the interested industrials"—and informing the company that a gunmakers' conference was to be held early in the following year "in order to consider the proposals of the different gun-producing centres, to elaborate a common programme and adopt a line of conduct to move the several Governments to amend the proposed convention. . . ." At the initial stages, the gunmakers pretended to be concerned, only with the unrestricted trade in "sporting arms and such for personal defence", but, as we shall see later, this was merely the thin end of a very thick wedge. At the end of their letter, the Liége committee pointed out that a similar communication had been directed to the English, French, Italian, Czechoslovakian, German, Austrian and Hungarian manufacturers.

Meanwhile, another American company—Colt's Patent Fire Arms—had been informed of the preparations for the Geneva Convention by *Fabrique Nationale d'Armes de Guerre* of Belgium,[1] in a letter which read, in part, as follows :—

"It is, of course, understood that our general interest is to prevent the hatching up of a new agreement plan. . . . We therefore consider that in order to lengthen the controversies (and to thus wear out in the long run the bodies occupied with this question) a very simple solution would be to lead your Government not to name representatives for the Temporary Mixed Commission, or at least (if your Government cannot consider the possibility of a categorical refusal) to delay the nominations just as long as possible. This matter presenting, for both of our companies, extreme importance, we do not doubt that on receipt of this letter you will wish to immediately get busy in the high places and have steps taken, without delay, along the above-mentioned line, using all the influence at your command. We are sending a similar request to the Remington Co."

[1] Colts and *Fabrique Nationale* were at that time linked together by a military sales agreement.

Within a month of the receipt of the Liége committee's letter Mr. Beebe, Winchester's foreign manager, wrote to the company's Washington representative :—

"It appears to me that our course of action should be to learn who will represent this Government at Geneva and then fully post such representative in regard to our goods, their uses, and the class of trade that buys them. . . . If you agree with this, will you kindly endeavour to find out who is going to represent the United States and suggest the best method of approach? Fortunately both Congressman Tilson[1] and Senator Bingham are military men (sic), and as I know them both I can take the matter up with them as soon as we hear from you. Doubtless we can also get some of the other manufacturers to take it up with their representatives."[2]

Shortly after the despatch of this letter, Mr. Beebe and Mr. Nichols (of Colts) paid a friendly visit in Washington to Congressman Tilson and Senator Bingham. They also had a cosy chat with General Ruggles of the War Department, who, by a happy coincidence, was subsequently appointed as a delegate to the Geneva Convention. At the same time, we find Mr. Beebe informing his company's Washington representative that "I have just received a letter from Congressman Tilson in which he states that Mr. Dulles, Chief of the Near Eastern Division of the State Department, called him on the phone and stated that he would like to talk over personally with me the proposed restriction of traffic in arms". Two months later the American public was informed that Mr. Dulles had also been nominated as a Geneva delegate.

Things were beginning to map out fine. On February 20, 1925, Mr. Beebe reported to his fellow armament manufacturers in the United States that "it would seem to us as if the control by sovereign States could be left to each importing State as at present. . . . This would, of course, leave the situation practically as it is today.

[1] Then Majority Leader in the House of Representatives.
[2] Nye Committee Hearings, Exhibit 818.

"As I see it," he added, "to bring this condition about would mean urging our Government *to decline to enter into any agreement to control the international trade of private manufacturers.* . . . If our Government does this, I feel sure that our representatives will be willing to give sympathetic consideration to such amendments as manufacturers in this country may suggest in the direction of removing the handicaps and prohibitions on the sale of arms and ammunition used primarily for hunting, sport, target practice, and ammunition, *and at the same time make less drastic the provisions applying to war munitions"* [our italics].[1]

In the same week, the Gunmakers' Congress was held in Paris. Drastic modifications of the proposed convention were agreed to unanimously by all sections of the Bloody International; the congress passed a resolution that the private manufacture of "war arms, ammunition and material must remain free" subject to national laws and peace treaties actually in force; that the gunmakers' desires should be made known to their respective Governments; that the Governments should add to their delegations experts thoroughly acquainted with the needs and desires of the gunmakers' trade and traffic, and—that these demands should not be communicated to the Press.

A full report of the proceedings was sent to the American companies, which, in March, 1925, managed to secure (without, we imagine, much difficulty) the co-operation of Mr. Herbert Hoover, then Secretary of Commerce. This new and formidable ally called an informal conference of armament manufacturers in Washington, invitations being sent to the Hunter Arms, Inc., Ithaca Gun Co., Winchester Repeating Arms Co., Remington Arms, Hercules Powder, United States Cartridge Co., Harrington & Richardson Arms Co., du Pont de Nemours, Colt Co., and Western Cartridge Co. The first meeting was a great success. Mr. Hoover started off by assuring the Merchants of Death that

[1] Nye Committee Hearings, Exhibit 823. In their report the Nye Committee suggested that Mr. Beebe had come to the conclusion that under the circumstances it would be less difficult and probably more successful for the arms manufacturers interested in the proposed convention to ask for the modification of the treaty rather than outright rejection of it. (Report no. 944, Part 3, p. 133.)

he was thoroughly opposed to any burdensome restrictions on American manufacturers. He then proceeded to read, one by one, the various articles of the draft convention—pausing, between whiles, to hear, and to signify his support of, the spirited objections raised against every article which carried the faintest promise of mitigating the evils of the Bloody Traffic. At the end of the meeting, Mr. Hoover advised the manufacturers to set up an executive committee which would prepare a final report to be submitted to him at a subsequent meeting.

This second meeting was held on April 14, and was attended by four of the United States representatives at the Geneva Convention—Mr. Dulles, General Ruggles, Major Strong and Admiral Long. Mr. Hoover told the gathering that the United States would have to agree to some form of licensing of arms exports, but that he intended to have a system whereby all U.S. customs commissioners *would have absolute instructions to issue licences automatically on presentation of a consular visa,* and that every effort would be made by the U.S. Government to eliminate red tape, delay or hindrance. In the case of some large military materials, such as heavy guns, battleships, etc., it *might* be necessary to refer to Washington, but even then every effort would be made to eliminate delay or annoyance to the manufacturer. Admiral Long stated that the United States delegation would not tolerate for a minute any plan which would in any way interfere with sea shipments, and the other delegates added their assurances that the main principles of the draft convention would be resolutely opposed at Geneva.[1]

The above minutes are taken from a confidential report[2] by Major Simons, an official of the du Pont Company and vice-chairman of the manufacturers' executive committee. The closing paragraph in this report reads:—

"With the reservation made by the United States Government and the presence at the conference of Admiral Long,

---

[1] It should be noted here that when a nation accepts an invitation to such a conference it is always understood that it accepts the general principles outlined for discussion.

[2] Nye Committee Hearings, Exhibit 837.

United States Navy; General Ruggles, United States Army; and Major Strong, United States Army, all of whom are familiar with our point of view, it is believed that the interests of the du Pont Co. and our customers will be properly looked after."

This paragraph, together with certain extracts from letters exchanged between the conspirators during the following six months, stands as a final epitaph to the ill-fated Geneva Convention. We reprint these extracts, without comment, from Part 9 of the Hearings of the Nye Committee, which subsequently investigated the operations of the arms traffic on behalf of the American Congress.

I

May 23, 1925. From Major Simons to Mr. Beebe:—

". . . It has been my belief all along that if we can insist on American reservations and insist particularly that this convention will not go into effect until ratified by all countries manufacturing arms and munitions, that we shall be safe from any interference for this generation at least."

II

May 26, 1925. From J. W. Harrington (Harrington and Richardson Arms Co.) to Mr. Beebe:—

". . . We have great confidence in our representatives and the present Secretary of State, and really feel that ultimately there will be no result from the Geneva Conference."

III

June 4, 1925. From Mr. Beebe to Congressman Tilson:—

". . . You may be sure that I appreciate what you have done in an effort to safeguard our interests. . . . In some newspaper articles there has been mention made of a possible successor to Secretary Weeks . . . and your name has been very prominently mentioned. . . . On the other hand, considering the responsible position that you hold in Congress, I can imagine that you might feel your opportunities for service were greater in your present position. This is just to let you know in a personal way that my own feeling is, there is nothing too good for 'John', if he wants it."

IV

July 20, 1925. From Major Simons to W. Talbot Penniman (Northern Giant Explosives, Ltd.):—

". . . In reference to our conversation regarding the International Convention on the Trade in Munitions, it may be of interest to you to hear that on my recent visit to Washington I saw a copy of the convention finally signed at Geneva, and it is not nearly as bad as we thought it was going to be. There will be some few inconveniences to the manufacturers of munitions in their export trade, but in the main they will not be hampered materially."

V

August 17, 1925. From Mr. Casey (du Pont) to Colonel W. N. Taylor (European representative of du Pont and Imperial Chemical Industries' predecessor, the Nobel Trust):—

", . . The net result of this conference does not appear to be disadvantageous to the munition manufacturers, since the new regulation requiring a formal permit to export munitions has had the effect of an official recognition of this trade by the United States State Department, so that they must hereafter give the same assistance and support to munition exporters as they would give to any other firms. Admiral Long quoted a conversation which he had had with some State Department official, wherein the State Department official stated that he regarded the munition manufacturers as deserving the same support that was given to exporters of sewing machines. . . . We understand further that the action of the chief of the American delegation, Mr. Burton, in regard to the prohibition of the use of poison gas was taken without consultation with the rest of the American delegation, and was regarded by the entire conference as a 'magnificent gesture', the actual wording of the accepted protocol leaving the nations at liberty to act pretty much as they see fit."

VI

August 27, 1925. From Major Simons to Mr. Beebe:—

". . . The action of the State Department in identifying itself with this business has put the State Department in the attitude of recognising this as being in the same category with other foreign commerce, or as one State Department official is said to have remarked, 'the export of munitions is as reputable as the export of sewing machines'. . . . Personally, I think that the Geneva Conference has had a great educational value for our State Department, no small part of which is due to your skilful and untiring presentation of the facts before these officers sailed for Europe. It has been a great pleasure for me to work with you in this matter and a greater pleasure still to compliment you on the results which you obtained."

VII

August 28, 1925. From Mr. Beebe to Major Simons:—

". . . I will admit I worked hard, but can assure you that any success that attended our efforts was due quite as much to you and my associates on the committee."

VIII

October 13, 1925. From Colonel W. N. Taylor to Mr. Casey:—

". . . Now that the conference of Geneva has more or less legalized the sale of American military goods abroad it seems to me well worth while to consider the possibility of American munition people getting together and making loans to these countries for substantial orders. The possibilities for big sales lies only along those lines. . . . The countries that at present would be willing to undertake loans of let us say $5,000,000 to $10,000,000 apiece would be: Poland, Czechoslovakia, Greece,

B 2

Roumania, Norway, Denmark, Finland. If such a thing were properly organized, it seems possible that within two years we could develop orders in Europe around $40,000,000,000 worth of material. I have an idea that there are plenty of banks that would put up the money if the total were big enough."

So ended the first attempt at international control of the Bloody Traffic.

We have described, in some detail, the manner in which the American delegates were briefed by the armament manufacturers —and their friends in the Government—to be *their* "mouthpieces" at a world conference called in the interests of the common people of all countries. What happened in America happened, no doubt, to a greater or lesser extent, in all the other arms-producing States represented at Geneva, but it is only in America that the full story has been exposed. The fate of the original draft convention was not, as is popularly believed, decided at Geneva. It was decided in the board-rooms of the armament combines and at "informal" departmental conferences sponsored by that type of Government minister to whom lucrative company directorships ultimately flow with such monotonous regularity.

"Star" of Bethlehem

Today the very word "disarmament" has an unreal, even sinister, import to the majority of people. We are all of us wise about disarmament—with the spurious wisdom that comes after the event. "Disarmament just does not work. It was tried, and it was a flop, and we can thank our lucky stars it did not come off." This sort of statement seems to represent the total degree of intellectual effort which the average man and woman—and, for that matter, the average politician and publicist—is prepared to exert when asked to pass judgement on the outstanding humanitarian experiment of this age. It is so easy to reiterate, parrot-fashion, the slick and shallow verdicts of the Penny-paper Historians: so tiresome to have to probe below the surface for the real influences behind the decay and collapse of the League's authority.

To see, in their true perspective, the events outlined in this, chapter, it is necessary to realize that there *was* a time when the great mass of the politically-conscious genuinely believed in the principle of world disarmament; were profoundly disturbed by the prospect of an international arms race, and entertained solid hopes that out of the Geneva conferences would emerge a sane and practical plan for ensuring world peace by collective security.

"The League", says Mr. Beverley Baxter, "persuaded the righteous to disarm and permitted the wicked to arm." [1] This is nothing more than the propitiatory rationalizing of a conscience-troubled Tory. Beverley Baxter knows very well that if the League stood for anything it stood for the principle and practice of *universal* disarmament; that the vitiation of this principle was brought about by the unholy alliance between the armament manufacturers and the imperialists and chauvinists of the Great Powers; that it is at their doorsteps that we must lay the greater part of the blame for the League's failure. Later we shall see how the "righteous"—by which Mr. Baxter can only mean the Governments and ruling classes of the Great Powers—not only permitted the "wicked" to arm but actively aided them *in direct contravention of the League Covenant and the Treaty of Versailles.*

At the height of the disarmament campaign, the Union of Democratic Control published *The Secret International*—a masterly indictment of the armament firms' anti-Geneva activities. The passage which follows is taken from the opening pages of this work, and will serve as an introduction to one of the greatest scandals of the inter-war years:—

"Today, almost everyone pays lip-service to the cause of disarmament. No one says in public that it would not be better if the nations spent less money and employed fewer men on the making of shells and guns, tanks and submarines, battle-ships and battle aeroplanes, in devising new and more deadly forms of poison gas and explosives. This pamphlet assumes general agreement about that. It also assumes that most people are bitterly disappointed that the progress towards a goal which

[1] *Evening Standard,* July 20, 1943.

is generally desired is so slow, and it suggests that one reason why it is so slow is that there is a very active and powerful force working nationally and internationally against disarmament.

"No doubt it is true that the greatest obstacles in the way of disarmament are the 'Unseen Assassins' of which Sir Norman Angell has written—the unreasoning nationalism that persists side by side with the nascent internationalism of the world, the greed for power that afflicts every organised political group, the fear that others will be more powerful, the unwillingness we all show to sacrifice the desire of the moment for long-distance ends. But those who have worked for the cause of disarmament during the last twelve years, those who study the attitude of the newspapers and even sometimes of government servants at critical moments during disarmament conferences, agree that they meet in many indirect ways an opposition which is secret and powerful, an opposition which is not internal but external, which does not spring from popular apathy towards disarmament but which is organized by those who have a financial interest in the upkeep of arms. This organization and propaganda against disarmament is itself international. Those who promote it are not patriots or nationalists; they are business men whose interests are to encourage inflated patriotism and national animosities. They aim not at the triumph of any particular nation but at selling as many munitions as possible. . . . Those who make arms live by the fears and hatred which lead to war. When war does come, they grow fat. The follies and divisions of mankind are their daily bread; the catastrophes which impoverish the world are their banquets. They prosper most when we mourn over a generation dead."

". . . *an opposition which is . . . external . . . organized by those who have a financial interest in the upkeep of arms . . . whose interests are to encourage inflated patriotism and national animosities*". This is stern language. Is it justified?

Let us take the case of Mr. Shearer and the Geneva Naval Conference of June, 1927.

To appreciate the general effect of Mr. Shearer's activities on behalf of American shipbuilding interests one must go back to the Washington Naval Conference of 1921. At that time the British Government faced the very real threat of losing its naval supremacy to America—which, alone of all the major Powers, commanded the resources necessary to the launching of a capital shipbuilding programme. On the face of it, therefore, the final agreement at Washington on a capital ship ratio of 5-5-3 as among Britain, America and Japan—proposed by Secretary of State Hughes and accepted by Lord Balfour, head of the British delegation—might have appeared as a grudging concession of equality to Britain's new rival for naval hegemony. In fact, the Washington pact was a triumph for British diplomacy. Equality in capital ships was assured, the American plans for large-scale construction of heavy battleships forcibly shelved *and Britain's overwhelming superiority in cruiser strength maintained.* The balance of naval power remained definitely with Britain.

And, all things considered, this was how it should be. With Empire lines and trade routes longer than those of any other country in the world, it was logical that she should require the greatest navy. A further advantageous feature of the Washington agreement was that it had the effect of limiting Japan's heavy ships to less than one-third of the Anglo-American total. True, Britain's refusal to accept cruiser limitation [1] left Japan with a free hand to concentrate on this type of vessel; but the Eastern Power's first real opportunity came with the breakdown of the Geneva Conference of 1927 and the consequent abandonment of *all* existing agreements. We will not attempt to apportion the blame for this breakdown. Suffice it to say that the American delegates pressed for complete paper parity, that the British delegates rejected these requests, and that the Japanese delegates went back to Tokyo grinning like Cheshire cats. As to the cause of the U.S. delegates' uncompromising attitude at Geneva— for that we must turn to the "external opposition organized by those who have a financial interest in the upkeep of arms"; in

[1] Ostensibly on the grounds that France would not agree to the abolition of submarines.

other words, to the "patriotic" shipping magnates of the United States.

At the time of the Geneva Naval Disarmament Conference, the three big U.S. shipbuilders had received contracts for $53,000,000 worth of work on six 10,000-ton cruisers. Newport News had received two ships at a contract price of $21,284,000, Bethlehem one ship at a contract price of $10,675,000 and New York Shipbuilding one of the new cruisers at $10,815,000 plus other contracts valued at $10,970,000. All these contracts could be cancelled as a result of action by the Geneva Conference. The three companies thus stood to lose £53,744,000 of work if the Geneva Conference prevented a naval race.

The Conference was held in June. In March of that year, representatives of the three companies met together and decided to hire the services of an "observer" to report to them on the developments at Geneva for a fee of £6,250. Shearer, the man chosen to execute these duties, had already proved his abilities as an "observer" by his work for the companies in connection with the above-mentioned cruiser contracts, as the following testimony (taken before a subsequent Senate Committee [1]) clearly shows:—

Mr. Shearer: They said, "We do not want a campaign through the country, but we want action right away". They said, "There is a cruiser bill in Washington, and unless we get $200,000 for the plans by June 1 it dies, according to law, and you go to Washington and see what you can do with it".

Senator Clark: In other words, the appropriation would lapse if they did not have it under contract at the end of the fiscal year.

Mr. Shearer: Absolutely; yes, sir. So that I came down to Washington.

Senator Vandenberg: What was the pay arrangement?

Mr. Shearer: $7,500, and they advanced me expenses.

Senator Clark: Was it at this time that you took a page in the *New York Commercial?*

[1] Senate Committee Print: Munitions Industry, Naval Shipbuilding, p. 236.

Mr. Shearer: No, I did not take it then. They wanted action on cruisers and not publicity.

Senator Clark: They made an arrangement with you for a flat fee to conduct this campaign?

Mr. Shearer: Yes, I would say that it was a flat fee.

Senator Clark: They would pay you $7,500 for coming down here and working for the cruisers?

Mr. Shearer: The three-cruiser program.

Senator Clark: The cruisers had already been authorized, had they not?

Mr. Shearer: Yes; but no appropriation; and, unless something is appropriated, they die according to law. So that down I came, and evidently they were satisfied because, on my return to New York, they asked me to go to Geneva.

Senator Clark: You got the cruisers?

Mr. Shearer: I would not say that. *They* got the cruisers.

Senator Clark: You accomplished your purpose?

Mr. Shearer: I got my $7,500 and they got the cruisers.

Senator Clark: Let us say, you got the cruisers for them.

Actually, these cruiser contracts were suspended pending the results of the Geneva Conference. Shearer's duties were clearly defined: he was to use his formidable powers as a publicist and scaremonger; his friendship with high-ranking U.S. naval officers; his close contacts with such so-called patriotic societies as the National Society of Daughters of the American Revolution, the National Defence League, the National Security League, etc., to one end—the prevention of any effective measures for cruiser limitation. In view of his somewhat unsavoury record as a lobbyist-cum-speakeasy-promoter-cum-bootlegger, it was imperative that his commission should not be brought to the notice of the State Department.

Senator Clark: What was the final upshot of that discussion? Did you go to Geneva openly as the representative of the ship-building companies?

Mr. Shearer: I went to Geneva but not openly, no, sir; as a representative of the three.

Senator Bone: Mr. Shearer, are you in any way ashamed of your business connection?

Mr. Shearer: Certainly not.

Senator Bone: Why did you keep your connection with these people secret?

Mr. Shearer: Because those people asked me to keep it secret.

Senator Bone: That throws a little light on the subject.

As with the previous conference on the control of the arms traffic, steps were taken to prejudice the minds of the U.S. delegates and other officials concerned before they had even been given an opportunity of hearing the arguments from the other side.

Asked to describe the atmosphere which prevailed in certain Washington circles immediately prior to June, 1927, Mr. Drew Pearson, then a Government official, said :—[1]

"The conversation in general was almost identical with Shearer's views, and was . . . extremely anti-British. It was also to the effect that the Washington Naval Conference [*of 1921*] had been a terrible failure; that Mr. Hughes had sacrificed American parity on the high seas for political purposes; and that they hoped, and would endeavour to see that the conference . . . would not succeed. They said, 'We are out to see that there is no repetition of 1921'. That was the thing in a nutshell. What struck me at the very start of the conference was that there was an atmosphere among these naval experts and Shearer that was extremely discouraging to the success of the conference. In other words, *the cards were stacked against the conference from the very start*.".

Mr. Shearer's subsequent activities are described in a letter written by himself to the representatives of the shipping companies on March 10, 1928, from which the following passages are extracted :—

". . . I sailed for France March 19, 1927, renewed my contacts in Paris, and arrived in Geneva, Switzerland, early in

[1] Hearings on S. 114, 71st Congress, 1st Session, p. 393.

April, renewing there my work at the Preparatory Arms Conference on disarmament . . . April 11, 1927, the Preparatory Arms Conference collapsed. From that date until June 20, 1927, I carried on a publicity campaign both in Europe and the United States; multigraphed articles were posted to the Press of Europe and the United States, Members of Congress and the Cabinet, patriotic societies, business men, and many others, including the Army and Navy. These many releases had wide publicity and became the instructive guide to all Press correspondents at Geneva. Many letters in my possession from the Press, patriotic societies and the American Legion acknowledge and substantiate that.

"This advance campaign and the accuracy and authentic data[1] released by me, automatically made me the leader of the unofficial fight to the extent that American officials referred the Press to me, as they were bound to secrecy, with the result that the attempt to deliver the United States was defeated by a complete exposé, which is now acknowledged.

"At the close of the Conference, August 4, 1927, the European press recognized and acknowledged the effect of my campaign, referring to it as 'the triumph of the theses of William B. Shearer, the American'.[2]

"I remained in Geneva until September 1, 1927, gathering information on the new line-up and the proposed plans to defeat the naval recommendations to go before the Seventieth Congress. . . . . September 1, 1927, I went to Italy for the purpose of learning the Italian attitude on future naval and marine activities, returning to France for the same purpose,

[1] As might be expected, Shearer always maintained, and appeared to be personally convinced, that the wretched conglomeration of lies, distortions and half-truths with which he launched his various campaigns represented the truth, the whole truth and nothing but the truth. Asked by Senator Clark to describe his *modus operandi*, he said: "I will tell you what it is. First you get the facts, and then you stick to the truth, and giving facts and truth the opposition never battles you down." Senator Bone: "That would be likely to ruin you in a fight of that kind, would it not?"

[2] The full passage, quoted elsewhere in the Senatorial hearings, was: "The triumph of the theses of William Shearer, the American, gave yesterday the drop of the barrier to the most formidable marathon of modern times. To-morrow the race of armaments will recommence."

then sailed September 29 for New York. . . . On October 3, 1927, I released my first story in all the Hearst Sunday papers. . . . My publicity campaign continued in all the Hearst papers, *Washington Post*, journals and weeklies along with considerable correspondence. . . . I have attended all hearings before the House Committee on Naval Affairs, and have advised certain patriotic societies in their campaign against the pacifists. . . . My entire time, energy and knowledge have been devoted 100% to the cause of the shipbuilding industry and sea power. . . . I have reasons to believe that the results of my consistent campaign and past endeavours have been and will be of great benefit to the shipbuilding industry, and all parties interested materially and otherwise."

The Big Three shipbuilders had every reason to be satisfied with Shearer's work at Geneva. Following the break-up of the conference, contracts were let for eight 10,000-ton cruisers proportionately divided between Bethlehem Shipbuilding, Newport News and American Brown-Boveri Electric Corporation and a seventy-one shipbuilding programme costing $740,000,000 was placed before Congress early in 1928. Shearer received a royal welcome on his return from Europe and, on the suggestion of the shipbuilders, installed himself in a house at Washington where he could keep a watchful eye on the Administration. Soon, however, a discordant note shattered the harmony of employer–employee relationships. On December 17, 1927, the £6,250 "Geneva" contract was formally terminated—the shipbuilders giving Shearer to understand that from now on he would be paid purely on a "commission" basis for work done and services rendered.

Shearer had other ideas. He knew that this sudden "pay-off" was dictated by the shipbuilders' very real fear that the full facts of the Geneva conspiracy would be brought to light. Deciding, very wisely, to capitalize this fear, he entered a claim for $200,000 —representing the total bonus "due" to him (at $25,000 a year) for the eight years of the projected shipbuilding programme. For a little while the Big Three managed to keep him quiet with one or two small commissions, but by February, 1928, his patience had become exhausted and on the 17th of that month we find him writing to the Vice-President of the Brown-Boveri company :—

". . . . The issue is not whether I am a German, which has been disproved, or whether I am socially qualified to associate with shipbuilders or something worse. The issue is whether the American Brown-Boveri Electric Corporation, the Bethlehem Shipbuilding Corporation and the Newport News Shipbuilding Co. benefited by my campaign. . . . You say I was to go to Geneva as an observer only. Every member of the shipbuilding group received my releases before, during and after the Coolidge Naval Conference at Geneva, and at no time was I instructed to change or stop my tactics. . . . All this was acknowledged and approved by the interested shipbuilding group until a small Navy paper, international and pacifistic in policy, asked the Navy Department for information about me. Then came the disavowal and damnation by the shipbuilders, accepting the fruits of victory but deserting the leader of the fight. I was to be made the victim of success, which was cowardly, contemptible and unjust. To carry out this ungrateful policy, my citizenship and character were attacked, not only to repudiate me but to rob me of my just reward and recognition which was promised. But defamation of character is not the real issue. I prefer to stick to the real issue, i.e., to receive a fair settlement based on fair equity as the result of my work, and on that I propose to lay this matter wide open on its merits; then personalities, reputations, characters and business ethics, which you have tried to make the issue, will have their innings. I am prepared to meet these issues in the same spirit of justice, fairness and firmness that has ever characterized my actions, and I am also prepared to support fully the position I assume."

Moved, we may assume, less by the eloquence of Shearer's denunciation than by the open threat contained in the last part of his letter, the shipping bosses kept him on their pay-roll until March, 1929. His work, in that period, showed no sign of having been adversely affected by the cruel blow which the Big Three had struck at his *amour propre* and his faith in human decency. If anything, bitterness and disillusionment served to sharpen his already highly-developed imaginative faculties, for, in the autumn of 1928, he managed to persuade all the important American papers to give editorial space to one of his most successful war scares, which took the form of a diary—captured, according to Shearer, from a British secret agent. The diary went over in a big way; which is not surprising, for it was written by the master himself.

Much valuable work was done during this period to keep before the public mind the ever-present "menace" of disarmament. The following extract, which is taken from a pamphlet written by Shearer on behalf of his employers, tells everything there is to know of this wretched lackey's propaganda methods and of the poor, diseased mentality from which they sprang:—

"From October, 1914, the weight of internationalism and communism was developed, the members of which, pacifists, defeatists, radicals of many hues, and foreign agents, communists, I.W.W. and socialists, included in this merger, and a dozen or more organizations with impressive names designed to fool patriotic Americans and lend aid to the enemy. Associated with these agents and organizations of these anti-American bodies were statesmen, senators, bankers, lawyers, actors, directors and writers, men and women of American birth who were used to fight the existing Government of the United States. . . . All names, records, cheques from prominent people in this country, instructions from Moscow, speeches, theses, questionnaires, indeed the workings of the underground organization, working secretly through 'legal' bodies in labour circles, in society, in professional groups, in the Army and Navy, in Congress, in the schools and colleges of the country, in banks and business concerns, among the farmers, in the motion-picture industry, in fact in nearly every walk of life—this information and authentic documentary proof of a colossal conspiracy against the United States were seized by Federal officials and are in possession of the authorities." [1]

[1] Senate Naval Affairs Committee Hearings, 71 : 1–2, pp. 599–600.

Needless to say, the author gives no clue as to the exact nature or identity of the "authentic" documents pertaining to the colossal conspiracy.

In the summer of 1928, Shearer appeared in the newspapers in another rôle—that of a worker demanding his just wages. The shipbuilders having rejected his final demand for $200,000, he sued for payment:—

"The public now became interested to know more about this strange alliance of patriotism and business. Senators and representatives and, most important of all, President Hoover, who had suffered from vitriolic attacks for his negotiations for disarmament, displayed curiosity. Senatorial investigation was decreed. It called Mr. Palen and Mr. Bardo, and Mr. Wilder, and Mr. Grace of the Bethlehem Steel Company and Mr. Grace's superior Mr. Charles A. Schwab—and it did not have to summon Mr. Shearer. He appeared voluntarily, eagerly, and insisted that he be heard.

"A strange spectacle followed. It was odd, indeed, to observe how these titans of American industry sought to portray themselves as bungling, inefficient executives, as innocent but stupid employers. It was extraordinary to observe how readily they admitted that they had employed a man about whom they knew nothing; and how they had sent him to Geneva for a task about the nature of which they had only the faintest idea—and that they had paid out $25,000 for this nebulous enterprise.

"Mr. Bardo was particularly vague as to why he had consented to the hiring of Mr. Shearer. He admitted that he knew nothing about the man, and conceded that by so doing he had violated one of the principal rules which he had always followed as an employer. He was equally obscure in his understanding of the objective which this strange employee was to work for. According to this president of the New York Shipbuilding Company, Shearer was sent to Geneva simply as an observer to report the 'trend' of the conference so that the shipbuilders would have more information than was available in the newspapers. The results of the conference, he declared, did not possess interest for him; the 'trend', not the 'result' was what he was interested in—whether the conference ended in an agreement or not.

"*Senator Robinson* of Arkansas (questioning Mr. Bardo): It (a failure) might aid you and yet you are interested in the trend but not the result.

"*Mr. Bardo:* But not in a disagreement. Please do not get those two terms confused. We were interested in the trend but not in a disagreement.

"*Senator Robinson:* You have made a distinction which I confess my poor mind is not able to grasp, but perhaps you will make the effort to explain just why you were interested in tending toward disagreement, but in no wise interested in disagreement itself.

"*Mr. Bardo:* Because one indicated a trend, the other indicated a result." [1]

The fine and meticulous distinctions made by armament magnate Bardo will perhaps be more comprehensible to the reader than they seem to have been to the inquiring Senator. The authors feel bound to confess that his far from disinterested niceties escape them.

BOMBERS' MOON

Turning from the realm of naval armament to aviation, we meet the same stories of large trusts, high rates of profit, semi-secret internationalism and public nationalism (professed at the same time) for the ever-holy cause of business and private gain. As in the case of heavy armaments, manufacturers of military aeroplanes supplied many other Governments and had factories in foreign countries. It did not seem to matter whom the planes were destined to destroy so long as the price was paid. One of the largest British firms of aircraft production—the Fairey Aviation Company—supplied military aeroplanes in time of peace to the Governments of Germany, Holland, Belgium, Portugal, Japan,

[1] The passages quoted are taken from *Merchants of Death* by Engelbrecht and Hanighen, pp. 213–215.

Greece, Argentina and Chile, and had works at Gossilies in Belgium as well as in this country. One of the largest American military aviation firms had an arrangement with the largest Japanese firm for the manufacture of aeroplane engines. Great contracts were made between countries soon to be enemies in the air, as in the field, and they industriously and profitably toiled to arm one another for the later conflict.

". . . Interrelation between foreign and home trade in armaments (I consider) as one of the most subtle and dangerous features of the present system of private production . . . for the more armaments are increased abroad the more they *must* increase at home."

This was the considered view of Admiral Lord Wester Wemyss as expressed in an official memorandum laid before the Admiralty in 1918, at which time he was the First Sea Lord. It did not take the manufacturers long to spread this traffic to the new air weapon, and a flourishing world trade in aeroplanes developed in the inter-war years.

Between wars, the attention of experts as well as laymen was focussed on the possible uses in destruction and in terrorization to which this new aerial weapon could be applied. As time went on instances were not lacking where aerial bombardment was used in warfare (the British Government, for instance, relied chiefly on the bomber to maintain "law and order" in outlying parts of the Empire, and the bombing of cities and civilians in Abyssinia and later in Spain brought the horrors and possibilities of air warfare much closer to the Western world). In consequence, the demand grew in Europe for some sort of agreement whereby the aerial bombing of civilians should be prevented in the event of a second major conflict. Long before the Abyssinian and Spanish wars had confirmed the fears of the more enlightened, the general feeling had been strong enough to make the question of air disarmament or control one of the principal problems of a conference at Geneva.

Small companies prior to the last war had grown into large aircraft manufacturing concerns in little over a decade, and their

interests lay heavily in the same direction as those of the armaments international. Small wonder, then, that the Disarmament
Conference at Geneva in 1933 stimulated so much open opposition in those Press and public circles which were largely influenced
by the aircraft producers. Mr. Noel Baker, Private Secretary to
the President of the Disarmament Conference, seemed to have no
doubts on the matter, for in his evidence before the Royal Commission on the Private Manufacture of and Trading in Arms presented on October 30, 1935, he said he was quite sure "that Mr.
Shearer's spiritual brothers were at work in the Conference". He
gave it as his view that if the British Government had come in on
the right side the general demand for internationalisation of
aviation and air disarmament on the part of the members of
the League of Nations would have been successful. In his own
words: "The Disarmament Conference very nearly came to
agreement on drastic measures of air disarmament combined with
the internationalization of civil aviation". He went on to say,
however, that forces had been at work which undermined the
aims of the Conference, and he specified two forces in particular
which "tended to educate air interests" towards thinking that disarmament and the League of Nations were all nonsense. These
two forces were the patriotic societies and the technical journals
devoted to aviation.

Of the former, none was in favour of or even interested in the
international solution of the problem of aerial armament and
warfare—though this problem was for so long a prime concern of
all the great Governments of the world. The first of these societies
was the National Aerial Defence Association, and there were
three members of its executive with direct interests in armament
firms; the chairman was also chairman of an aircraft production
firm. The aims of another famous society, the Air League of the
British Empire, included "the establishment of a thriving aircraft
industry". The Secretary General of the Air League came to his
post from the boards of Vickers Aviation Limited and Super-
marine Aviation Limited. The Hands Off Britain Air Defence
League asked no subscription from its members but, judging
from the scale of its activities and propaganda, the organization

never lacked ample funds. Where did they come from? Their source has never been made public, but an interesting incident was referred to by Mr. Noel Baker in his evidence to the Royal Commission mentioned above. He quotes from *The Times* dated January 14, 1927:—

"The Air League of the British Empire has received an offer, on behalf of those interested in production, of £5,000 a year for two years under certain conditions, this sum to be used in organization and propaganda . . . yesterday the Executive Committee of the Air League . . . resolved to recommend to the postponed annual general meeting that the offer of £5,000 per annum for two years, in accordance with the undertaking given by Mr. Handley Page in his letter to Lord Burnham of December 17, 1926 . . . be accepted."

This may help the reader to understand why the Executive Committee of the Air League so assiduously pursued the "aim" quoted above of establishing a "thriving aircraft industry", and was even persistent enough to intervene successfully with the Government department concerned to alter the system of ordering used in 1933 on the grounds that it did not give the manufacturers a chance "to run their businesses on economical bases".

Naturally these Societies were interested in the expansion of flying and, as Mr. Noel Baker says, "the Air League carried on a campaign in favour of air bombing when many Governments were proposing its abolition".

The technical journals devoted to aviation, like most periodicals, depend largely upon advertising revenue—almost exclusively derived from the aircraft industry. It is not unnatural, therefore, that their policy usually reflects quite closely what the aircraft producers are thinking. Here are some of their comments on the Disarmament Conference, where our Government representatives, along with the accredited statesmen of the world, were trying to come to some agreement on the problem of aerial disarmament:—

I

". . . In military aviation everything points to real activity in the workshops in the near future. It will begin when the Disarmament Conference goes to pieces, as it most certainly will. Great Britain, having showed willingness by leading the way in partial practical disarmament . . . will proceed to arm herself. It is about time. . . ." (*Popular Flying*, December, 1933.)

II

". . . within the next few weeks the Disarmament Conference at Geneva will come to an end, and it will almost certainly end without any agreement to disarm—which will be the best end it could have." (*Aeroplane*, October, 1934.)

III

". . . now that the disarmament talk at Geneva is nearly done, there may be some chance of building a still bigger framework for our own Air Force." (*Aeroplane*, July, 1934.)

IV

". . . and now that money is easier we can afford to re-arm the whole Air Force every four or five years." (*Aeroplane*, July, 1934.)

Mr. W. Arnold-Forster, in his evidence before the Royal Commission on the Arms Traffic, pointed out that between October, 1933, and the early months of 1934 the *Daily Mail*, followed by the *Daily Mirror*, was conducting a campaign in favour of a large increase of the British Air Force. Between October 2, 1933 and March 31, 1934, the market prices of the shares of the six principal companies making aircraft had appreciated on an average by 70%. The returns at Somerset House dated January 12, 1934, show that at that time Daily Mirror Newspapers, Limited, held 4,000 shares in Fairey Aviation Co., Ltd.

In an article by the editor of *Aeroplane* in the issue for January

17, 1934, there is a clear explanation of why these journals continued this type of propaganda. In the editor's own words: ". . . the greatest amount of trade done by the British Aircraft industry, *on which the existence of this paper depends*, is done either with the Air Ministry, in supplying materials for the Royal Air Force, or with the Governments of foreign nations in war machines". (The italics are ours.) Thus the policy of the reduction of offensive armaments—a policy which was the avowed and agreed aim of the great Powers, whatever their objections in fact to the various practical proposals they discussed—spelt disaster to the aviation periodicals.

Dr. Hugh Dalton (now Minister of Economic Warfare) said in a speech on February 11, 1938, when speaking on the Disarmament Conference:—

"On February 10, in the first debate of the Conference, Italy proposed the abolition of all bombing planes. Germany, Russia and other States supported. The United States of America was friendly to the idea, and in June . . . definitely came out in favour. From the first, Sir John Simon and Lord Londonderry resisted and obstructed; and on July 7 Lord Baldwin, on behalf of the Government, opposed the abolition and proposed instead that limits should be defined within which air bombing should be legitimate. The consequences of that success are written in letters of blood in China, Abyssinia and Spain. And maybe the end is not yet."

The whole of the civilized world knows only too well now that "the end is not yet".

In the issue of the *Aeroplane* for July 18, 1934, appeared an advertisement of a military aeroplane. At that time the British Government was still contesting Germany's right to have any air force at all, and some nine months earlier the League of Nations had passed a resolution denouncing Germany for re-arming in violation of her international obligations. Only a few days later Mr. Baldwin made a speech announcing the formation of forty-one new squadrons needed to meet the air menace from Germany. The advertisement referred to above carried a picture.

of a military plane produced for export by the advertising company. *It bore the sign of the swastika.*

In his evidence to the Royal Commission, Mr. Noel Baker gave an example of the system of private sale of aeroplanes by British firms to Germany in 1934. He said: "Mr. McKinnon Wood has pointed out that, as the result of this sale, the German Government, whose competition is now forcing His Majesty's Government greatly to increase the British Air Force, obtained the benefits of prolonged research and experimentation carried out by a British Government Department at a very heavy expenditure of public money."

It must be abundantly clear that the interests of the private manufacture and sale of arms are the increase of profits. These interests cannot, in the nature of things, coincide with the interest of the nation and the world, which is security. Such activities as those outlined above must of necessity continue just so long as the interest of profit is allowed to run counter to the best interests of the community at large.

CHAPTER IV

"GIVE US THIS DAY OUR LITTLE WAR"

WE HAVE already had occasion to refer to evidence taken before the United States Nye Committee. Since we intend, in this chapter, to confine ourselves almost exclusively to facts brought to light as a result of the Nye investigation, a few words on the factors leading to the appointment of the committee, its composition, terms of reference, etc., would perhaps not be out of place.

On June 27, 1930, the Seventy-first Congress, responding to the long-standing demands of American war veterans for legislation "to take the profit out of war", created a War Policies Commission, which reported recommendations on December 7, 1931, and March 7, 1932, to decommercialize war and to equalize the burdens imposed by war on the various sections of the community. For more than a year, these recommendations were pigeon-holed by the Republican administration headed by President Hoover. The defeat of the Republican Party and Franklin D. Roosevelt's election as President coincided, however, with a fresh stiffening of popular feeling against the Merchants of Death, and in the summer of 1934 Congress, on the initiative of Miss Dorothy Detzer, secretary of the Women's International League, approved the appointment of a special committee to investigate the munitions industry.

The chairman of the committee was Senator Gerald Nye, the other six members being Senators W. F. George (Georgia), B. C. Clark (Missouri), H. T. Bone (Washington), J. P. Pope (Idaho), A. H. Vandenburgh (Michigan) and W. W. Barbour (New Jersey). The terms of reference were wide and generous,[1]

---

[1] Nye Committee's terms of reference were as follows:—

(a) To investigate the activities of individuals, firms and associations and of corporations and all other agencies in the United States engaged in the manufacture, sale, distribution, import or export of arms, munitions or other implements of war; the nature of the industrial and commercial organizations engaged in the manufacture of or traffic in arms, munitions or other implements of war; the quantities of arms, munitions or other implements of war imported into the United States, and the countries of and the committee was authorized to seize any books, papers and documents in the possession of the armament companies which might be of value to the inquiry and to subpoena and place on oath "such witnesses as it deems advisable".

Gerald Nye, realizing that the success or failure of his commission depended on his gaining access to the files of the armament manufacturers before they had grasped the full implications of Senate Resolution 206, struck swiftly and effectively. When the hearings commenced on September 4, 1934, the Nye Committee had in its possession copies of confidential letters and reports seized from the offices of every important company concerned in the inquiry. It would be quite impossible to over-state the part which these papers played in the resounding success of the Nye investigation. They revealed the whole sordid story of the arms merchants' activities from the close of the Great War, laying bare to the public eye an organized conspiracy against peace which struck deep at the roots of contemporary complacency and left an indelible imprint on the consciousness of an entire generation. Of prime importance was the fact that these documents produced a situation in which the manufacturers, *already condemned from their own mouths and pens*, were forced from the outset to *defend* themselves before the committee. This situation, it should be noted, was completely reversed at the abortive Royal Commission inquiry held in this country

---

origin thereof, and the quantities exported from the United States and the countries of destination thereof; and

(*b*) To investigate and report upon the adequacy or inadequacy of existing legislation, and of the treaties to which the United States is a party, for the regulation and control of the manufacture of and traffic in arms, munitions or other implements of war within the United States, and of the traffic therein between the United States and other countries; and

(*c*) To review the findings of the War Policies Commission . . .

(*d*) To inquire into the desirability of creating a Government monopoly in respect to the manufacture of armaments and munitions and other implements of war, and to submit recommendations thereon.

For the purpose of this resolution, the committee or any sub-committee thereof is authorized to hold hearings, to sit and act at such times and places during the sessions and recesses of Congress until the final report is submitted, to require by sub poena or otherwise the attendance of such witnesses and the production of such books, papers and documents, to administer oaths, to take such testimony and to make such expenditures as it deems advisable . . .

: (Details of permitted limits of expenditure, etc., follow here.)

eight months later, when the Big Bosses of the British armament combines, spared by an indulgent Government the indignities visited on their American colleagues, were in a position to bully and bluster their way through the necessarily sketchy and for the most part purely circumstantial evidence laid before the lukewarm Commission by private individuals and anti-war organizations.[1]

It is interesting that the seizure of the U.S. companies' documents, which were to play such a vital part in exposing the flagrantly anti-social nature of the armament companies' activities, evoked shrill protests from the British manufacturers' representatives in the House of Commons. In an attempt to denigrate the Nye Committee during the Commons debate on the private trading in arms on November 8, 1934, Sir Jonah Walker-Smith pointed out, with some heat, that "unlimited money is placed at the disposal of those conducting the [Nye] inquiry"; that the documents had been "impounded by gangster methods", and that they were examined in the absence of those who had been particularly concerned in the impounded correspondence. This Tory apologist was singularly uninformed (to put it kindly) on all three accounts. In the first place, the

[1] By comparison with the Nye Committee's terms of reference, those of the Royal Commission are laughable. Here they are:—

(1) To consider and report upon the practicability and desirability (both from the national and international point of view) of the adoption (a) by the United Kingdom alone, (b) by the United Kingdom in conjunction with other countries of the world, of a prohibition of private manufacture of and trade in arms and munitions of war, and the institution of a State monopoly of such manufacture and trade.

(2) To consider and report whether there are any steps which can usefully be taken to remove or minimize the kinds of objections to which private manufacture is stated in Article 8 (5) of the Covenant of the League of Nations to be open.

(3) To examine the present arrangements in force in the United Kingdom relative to the control of the export trade in arms and munitions of war and to report whether these arrangements require revision, and, if so, in what directions.

It will be noticed that the Commission was given no power to enforce the production of companies' files and documents or to administer the oath to witnesses. *The Financial News* was thus able to report, on September 12, 1934, that:—

"Foreign countries placing orders will feel assured that, here, at least, their orders will be executed in strict accordance with the law and *there will be no danger that their confidential correspondence will be broadcast.*".

Nye Committee was strictly limited to a maximum expenditure of $15,000. Secondly, if the committee's methods were those of the gangster, then the whole of the Seventy-third. Congress— democratically elected by the people of the United States— stands condemned for initiating the alleged crimes perpetrated by the committee. Walker-Smith's third allegation is effectively refuted by the voluminous records of the Nye hearings, which show that every document produced during the inquiry was examined in the presence of the various companies' representatives, who were given every opportunity to explain away their written indiscretions.

Walker-Smith's alarm at the outrages committed on the U.S. manufacturers' private filing-cabinets will be better appreciated when it is pointed out that he was associated with Vickers, and that some very revealing letters from Sir Charles Craven (Vickers' chief) were exhibited during the Nye hearings. Other eminent critics of the Nye Committee were Sir John Simon and Sir Austen Chamberlain, both of whom have figured on the shareholders list of Imperial Chemical Industries, whose chairman—Lord McGowan—came in for some other unfavourable publicity during the course of the inquiry.[1]

From the outset, Gerald Nye's committee came into conflict with powerful, hostile influences which, if they had had their way, would have squashed the inquiry before any real damage could be done to the reputation of the armament manufacturers. Pressure was brought to bear on Army and Navy chiefs, senators, high Administration officials—even on Mr. Cordell Hull—to have the inquiry suspended on the grounds that important trade secrets would be revealed to the world and that U.S. manufacturers would lose the confidence of overseas customers. Protests were lodged at Washington by British authorities anxious to "protect the interests" of the big British combines implicated in the course of the Nye hearings. Organized voting blocs throughout the country, such as the American Legion, the Catholics and the Middle-West farmers, were canvassed by arma-

---

[1] To his credit, Sir John Simon immediately disposed of the shares as soon as his attention was called to the matter.

ment interests and warned . that America's national defence was jeopardized, that the investigation would be capitalized by communists and other "anti-social" elements, that private enterprise and free competition were imperilled.

Gerald Nye's reaction to all such threats and solicitations can be gauged by the following extract taken from the *New York Times* of September 10, 1934 :—

"The public study into the huge du .Pont's affairs is being made over objections by Irenee du Pont, 'head of the century-old concern. His criticism of the committee some months ago irritated several members who sharply answered him. Chairman Nye announced that he had refused the du Pont demand that its trade secrets be withheld from the Press.

" 'These munitions makers have been doing business secretly for so long that it is about time their affairs were made public,' he continued. 'The very fact that protests have come from abroad shows the necessity for continuing. The inquiry will go on.' "

The executives of E. I. du Pont de Nemours & Co. had every reason for wishing to keep the American public in the dark as to its trade secrets. Between 1913 and 1918, the assets of this mammoth powder-manufacturing organization had expanded from $74,000,000 to $308,000,000, and its profits rose from $4,997,773 in 1914 to $43,098,075 in 1918. At the end of the first year of peace, the du Pont assets had fallen by $68,000,000 to $240,000,000 and net profits had slumped to $17,682,992. Peace, and the consequent suspension of Government war orders, brought relief from suffering and stringency .to millions of ordinary people throughout the world : to those who had thrived on war it brought reduced earnings, gloom and despondency.

In common with all other munition manufacturers, du Pont was obliged to turn its attention to foreign fields and to attempt, by the organization of a militant sales force, to stimulate war orders from those nations which were either without domestic munitions factories or whose productive capacity was incommensurate with the expansionist designs of the ruling parties.

C

In the words of Mr. K. K. V. Casey, du Pont's Director of Sales:—

". . . Knowing that it would probably be some time before we could possibly expect any business from the Government, we began this attempt abroad; and we were just like children in the wilderness when we started."[1]

Casey's sober estimate that it would be "some time" before the United States became involved in a second world war has been vindicated by subsequent events; but there is little in the events of the inter-war years to justify the picturesque analogy applied to his salesmen. Indeed, the "children" of those years were surely the common man and woman and that minority of democratic leaders who groped, blind and insensate, through the wilderness of rumours, antagonisms and apprehensions created by the Merchants of Death and their legions of commission-men.

The South American republics were the first to receive the attention of the peace-stricken arms companies. This sunny continent, with its thousands of miles of land frontiers and its impulsive, easily-roused peoples, had been spared the physical and financial depredations which four years of war had brought to the nations of Europe and Asia. There was nothing of Europe's intense preoccupation with intra-national affairs to deter the strong nationalist parties which dominated the South American political scene, and disputes over boundaries and commercial facilities soon became of frequent occurrence.

At first, these disputes amounted to no more than a blowing off of political steam accompanied, at odd intervals, by sporadic armed clashes and border "incidents". None of the nations concerned really wanted to fight and spill blood over their differences; nor, it must be confessed, did any of them show any marked willingness to settle their real or imagined grievances at the conference table. But whereas the general aversion from the violence and destructiveness of war sprang from simple, humanitarian roots, it became increasingly clear, as the years went by, that the intransigence of the various ruling parties was

[1] Nye Hearings, Part 5, p. 1149.

bolstered up to no small extent by such purely artificial considerations as the availability of armaments and the state of the nation's finances.

A militarily weak nation with a depleted treasury usually exercised a commendable restraint in its diplomatic relations with a more powerful neighbour. But let it succeed in floating a large foreign loan, and let it apply a large part of the resultant funds in the purchase of modern field guns, and a new note entered into these relations. Suave, "peace-loving" politicians and mild-mannered generals were transformed, overnight, into ranting demagogues and blustering militarists; long-forgotten disputes were regurgitated from Press, platform and pulpit; diplomatic restraint went by the board and threats, warnings and ultimatums became the order of the day.

This was the atmosphere, the political climate, that prevailed in most of the capitals of South America from the late 'twenties to the early 'thirties, and it was in this fear-racked, suspicion-torn continent that the "lost children" of the armament companies found their spiritual home. Their mission was simple and clearly defined. It was to stimulate war orders from the potential belligerents on as large a scale as possible. War and the preparation for war were the immediate concern of these commission men and sales managers; and every artifice—ranging from well-placed bribes to the age-old device of the "war scare" —was employed towards these ends. Peace, arbitration and reconciliation were, of course, also their concern, and the same bag of tricks served to defeat any moves in this direction.

It is difficult for the layman fully to appreciate the extent of the atrophy which years of armament trading brings to the social consciences of the Merchants of Death and their satellites. For example, how many readers would not interpret the first sentence in the following passage, isolated from its context, as an attempt at dry humour on the part of the author? The passage is extracted from a letter sent, on August 6, 1928, to Sir Charles Craven of Vickers-Armstrongs. In it Mr. L. Y. Spear, Vice-President of the Electric Boat Co. of America, wrote:—[1]

[1] Nye Hearings, Part 1, exhibit 127. (Our italics.)

"It is too bad that the pernicious [sic] activities of our State Department have put the brake on armament orders from Peru by forcing the resumption of formal diplomatic relations with Chile. My friends advise me that this gesture means that all contemplated orders must go over until next year. *This hitch also means that we must not delay too long in getting Aubrey* [the company's South American representative] *back on the job in Lima.* The indications are now that he ought to be there about January 1, 1929, which means that his private arrangements will have to be made quite soon."

THE SOUTH AMERICAN WAY

Before proceeding to an examination of the business relations between Vickers and Electric Boat, let us make quite sure that the Vickers chief fully shared his American colleague's belief that the nations of the world should be given free rein in a mad race for armaments. Two passages from letters[1] written by Sir Charles Craven to Mr. L. Y. Spear between October, 1932, and January, 1933, will suffice:—

". . . I think the position will turn out as follows: (1) We shall receive a firm contract [from the Admiralty] for one submarine about the third week in November. (2) . . . we shall receive a letter telling us that the Admiralty accept our price for the second submarine on the distinct understanding that . . . they can have the right to cancel the second one without any payment. All that you and I gain by the transaction will be that we shall know that if the ship is built Vickers will get the order. *If, on the other hand, Geneva or some other fancy convention decide that large submarines have to be abolished . . . the Admiralty can then retire gracefully without having to pay us anything.*"

And, in a second letter:—

". . . In other words, they [the Admiralty] will have the right to withdraw their promised order for the second ship if

[1] Nye Hearings, Part 1, exhibits 22 and 23. (Our italics.)

Geneva *or any other troublesome organization* upsets the large submarine." !

The business relations between Vickers-Armstrong and the Electric Boat Co. merit more than the summary treatment to which the scope of this book limits us, for they present a first-class illustration of the profit-sharing, territory-dividing technique outlined in Chapter II.

While Vickers manufacture armaments of all descriptions, the activities of Electric Boat are largely confined to the building of submarines. All agreements between the two companies were thus restricted to the building of and trading in these vessels.

One of the pioneers of the submarine, the Electric Boat Co., took early steps to have its basic patents protected in every country of the world. These patents covered certain inventions indispensable to the equipment of the modern submarine, and when the directors of Vickers decided to branch out into the construction of this particular type of craft they were obliged to turn to the American company for permission to use its patents. Electric Boat struck a hard bargain. It granted Vickers a licence to use its patents on the condition: (1) that it received 40% of all net profits earned from submarines built in Vickers' British shipyards, and (2) that it received 50% of all net profits earned from boats built, under the Vickers licence, in any other British or Continental yards after deduction of the profits allowed to the building firm. During the Nye hearings it was revealed that, over the past twenty years, the American company had received an average "rake-off" of £28,467 on every boat built by Vickers for the account of the British Government.

It is a testimony to the close co-operation between Vickers and the Admiralty that, on the day following the disclosure of this agreement by the Nye Committee (September 4, 1934), Sir Charles Craven was able to announce in London that the British Government fully approved the arrangement between his company and Electric Boat regarding submarine construction and that the agreement "had been drawn up five years ago with the full knowledge of the British Government". This may be reconcilable with a passage in a letter sent by Craven to Electric Boat on July 30, 1932, in which he wrote:—[1]

"May I suggest that even in code it is better not to mention any names of ships, as I am rather afraid that such telegrams might get into the hands of our clients, and it would be awkward if they asked me about our agreement with you. I am sure you will appreciate what I mean."

SENATOR NYE: "Is the conclusion to be drawn from that statement that the British Admiralty had no knowledge of the agreement between Vickers and you?"

MR. GARSE (*President of Electric Boat*): "I think that is what Mr. Craven means, that the British Admiralty might raise some objection to an American concern receiving any money on account of business with the British Government."[2]

To the best of our knowledge, the interpretation put upon the passage by Senator Nye has never been publicly challenged by Craven.

The agreement for the division of sales territory was as clearly defined as the profit-sharing agreement and showed the same tender regard for the "sacred" principles of private competition and free enterprise. The territory reserved exclusively for Vickers was Great Britain and the Empire, "including self-governing territories such as Canada, Ireland, Australia and India" (*sic*). Exclusively reserved for Electric Boat were the United States, "colonies and dependencies thereof, Republic of Cuba and all communities and countries governed by or under the suzerainty of the United States". Both companies were free to act "in all other countries of the world"—with the exception of Spain, Japan, France, Italy, Belgium, Holland, Norway, Finland, Brazil, Argentina and Peru and all dependencies and colonies of these countries. The last-named territories, where sales were subject to specific profit-sharing agreements between the two companies, comprised practically every country outside British and American suzerainty which was capable of buying,

[1] Nye Hearings, Part 1, exhibit 21.
[2] Nye Hearings, Part 1, page 30.

interested in buying, or permitted to buy submarines. In certain of these countries Electric Boat had licensees or was about to build submarines on its own account and did not want British competition. In the remainder Vickers had long-established agreements with domestic armament concerns, such as Mitsubishi of Japan, or owned large shareholdings in local subsidiary companies, such as the Sociedad Española Construccion Naval of Spain.

At the date on which we find Spear complaining to Sir Charles Craven of the State Department's "pernicious" interference in Peru–Chile relations, Vickers and Electric Boat had been working together in a world-wide control of basic submarine designs and patents for a quarter of a century.[1] This system of co-partnership produced advantages other than the obvious ones inherent in any scheme for profit-sharing, price-rigging and the elimination of independent outside competition. For example, it enabled the two companies to take sides in the Peru–Chile disputes. Vickers' sales to Chile stimulated counterbalancing orders by Peru. These orders were fulfilled by the Electric Boat Co., which was thus able to pocket the profits from the Peruvian orders *plus* the usual royalty on Vickers' sales to Chile.

To gain a clear picture of this submarine cartel's activities in South America it is necessary to go back to 1920, when the Washington representative of Electric Boat reported to his office that Admiral Niblack, Chief of Naval Intelligence of the U.S. Navy, had told him that

"the whole balance of power has been destroyed by Chile getting six submarines and two warships from England; and that it has caused a good deal of uneasiness on the part of the Argentine, *while Peru is absolutely helpless.*"[2]

The directors of Electric Boat decided forthwith that honour, chivalry and common decency compelled them to go to the aid of Peru. The fact that the Peruvian President then in office showed little inclination to throw his country into a naval race which could only end in war or national bankruptcy was a minor

[1] Senate Report no. 944, Part 3, p. 82.
[2] Nye Hearings, Part 1, exhibit 56. (Our italics.)

obstacle easily. overcome.. As early as March, 1919, Electric Boat had been negotiating with ex-President Leguia—a militarist and a chauvinist who had shown certain favours to the company before he was overthrown and forced to flee to Europe. His successor, who was more concerned with safeguarding his country's economic stability than acquiring expensive armaments, had, on attaining office, cancelled outright a contract made by his predecessor for the supply of Electric Boat submarines.

A *coup d'état*, carried out by a signally well-armed and adequately financed group of revolutionaries, brought the return to power of President Leguia,[1] and the stage was set for a resumption of the cordial business relations so rudely broken off by his predecessor. The fact that the United States Government had decided, as a matter of policy, not to supply from its own yards any war vessels to Peru or Chile, on the grounds that this would encourage an outbreak of war between the two countries, redounded to the advantage of Electric Boat. On June 1, 1920, Spear was able to inform the president of his company that, as a result of the United States Government's refusal to make a direct sale of war vessels to the Peruvian authorities, the company's own submarine proposals were "receiving favourable consideration". In the last paragraph of his letter,[2] Spear added :—

"It is reported on good authority that the British Government is going to help the Chileans out; and if this is so *or believed to be so* by the other Government [Peru] it ought to influence them in favour of our proposals."[3]

However questionable the ethics behind this reasoning might be, its logic was unassailable. A good general is one who believes that Fortune will smile on his plans provided his plans do not rely on Fortune. And so it was in 1920 that a certain Captain Aubry—then Naval Attaché to the Peruvian Embassy in

[1] Augusto Leguia remained in power until August, 1930, when he was forced to resign. He took refuge in a warship, but was detained, and finally transferred to the obscurity of a Peruvian prison.

[2] Nye Hearings, Part 1, exhibit 54.

[3] Asked by Senator Clark, on the first day of the Nye hearings, if it made any difference to his company whether it was true *or only believed to be true* by the Peruvian Government that Chile was arming, Spear replied, "Not a bit".

Washington—hired a theatre in Lima, the capital of Peru, and delivered a lecture, illustrated by some fifty lantern slides, on the superiority of the products of the Electric Boat Co. over all other submarines. The lecture was attended by 3,000 people, including the President and the Minister of Marine, and was subsequently published in book form and circulated all over South America.

"It appears", wrote an Electric Boat official to Spear on July 16, 1920,[1] "that Captain Aubry arrived in Lima at a most opportune time. The Minister from Italy had been active with the Society of the Pro-Marine and a contract had been prepared and was ready for signature calling for the purchase of three of the Laurenti [an Italian company] boats. If the contract had been signed it would undoubtedly have committed the country to that particular type of boat, but owing to the representations made by Captain Aubry, the contract was not signed and I judge a good deal of a hornet's nest was started which resulted ultimately in the action of the President and his Cabinet determining to order four submarine boats from the Electric Boat Co."

Aubry's friends thought he was crazy—spending all this money in boosting the sales of a company in which he had not a dollar's worth of interest. But Aubry just laughed—and laughed—and laughed, because, not long afterwards, he was able to resign his under-paid post as a naval attaché and take up an appointment as Electric Boat's South American agent at an annual income rising from $7,000 in 1923 to $45,847 in 1927.

With President Leguia back in power, his son Juan on the company's pay-roll, and the peripatetic Aubry scheming and intriguing in all the important capital cities of South America, business soon began to flourish. In 1924, Aubry secured an order for two more submarines, which involved local bribes of $15,000 per boat,[2] and in 1926 came an order for a further two boats, bribes this time totalling $12,000.[3]

[1] Nye Hearings, Part 1, exhibit 57.
[2] Senate Report no. 944, Part 3, p. 83.
[3] *Ibid.*, p. 84.

C 2

Meanwhile, Vickers was playing its part in Chile with equal vigour if somewhat less obvious success. In 1927, when Electric Boat was engaged in building two submarines for Peru, the American company was informed by its Chilean representative that Chile was in the market for two modern submarines. Relations between these two countries were then strained almost to breaking point over the Tacna–Arica dispute, and Spear, thinking very wisely that "it would not look very well for us to be dealing with the Chileans at the same time we were dealing with the Peruvians",[1] cabled Sir Charles Craven asking him to quote on the business. The third and fourth paragraphs of Spear's confirmatory letter[2] to the Vickers Chief are worth reproducing in full :—

"This is an appropriate time for me to tell you that none of us here have ever met our Chilean representative and consequently we cannot in any way vouch for his reliability. We all know, however, that the real foundation of all South American business is graft and it may well be that he knows the proper people to pay in Santiago. At any rate, I am passing the thing along to you for such action as you may think it proper to take, having in view your own separate negotiations. If you should decide to submit a tender now for two 'L' boats, with premium for early delivery, you will, of course, have to reserve our 5% royalty as well as the 5% commission referred to in the cable. On the other hand, if your decision is in the negative, you will have to be careful in the future if you should, on your own account, offer the 'L' type, since under such circumstances our Santiago man might very well come forward with a claim for commission.

"Please cable me your decision and action so that I can advise Santiago. In conclusion, I would like to add a little unsolicited and perhaps superfluous advice, which is that I would not be too modest about the price and would cover into it a substantial amount in excess of the 10% above referred to,

---

[1] Nye Hearings, Part 1, p. 8.
[2] *Ibid.*, exhibit 68.

my own experience being that at the last minute *something extra is always needed to grease the ways.*"

A month after Spear had complained of the "pernicious inter-ference of the State Department", we find Craven informing his American colleague that he is "trying to ginger up the Chileans to take three more boats" and asking him if he would accept the same royalty "as last time".[1]

Unfortunately for the submarine cartel, the naval race between Peru and Chile did not result in war. Indeed, with Leguia's final overthrow in 1930, relations between the two countries improved considerably.

The activities of the Merchants of Death elsewhere were, however, already being crowned with success. Hostilities between Bolivia and Paraguay over the Chaco territory broke out in 1928, intermittent guerrilla fighting continuing until 1932, when organized warfare began. Two years of warfare between Colombia and Peru over the Leticia territory also began in 1932.

PISTOL-PACKING PREACHER

We shall endeavour, in the remainder of this chapter, to confine ourselves to a purely factual account of the armament companies' activities in South America from 1928 to 1934. We shall build up an indictment solely on the basis of evidence supplied by the Governments of Britain and America; by a commission of the League of Nations, and by letters exchanged between officials and agents of the companies involved. As the story unfolds, the reader will find these companies condemned, out of their own mouths, as hardened war-mongers and in-veterate enemies of peace and international comity. The apologists for the system of private manufacture constantly assert that the activities of these Merchants of Death are confined to "catering to a demand which would otherwise be satisfied by foreign competitors". The reader will judge for himself how false and utterly evasive all such attempts at justification are proved to be in the light of the plain, unvarnished facts. If

[1] Nye Hearings, Part 1, exhibit 124.

he is not already convinced that the armament traders, by their very nature, *must* want war, *must* take an active part in fomenting war and, when war has come, *must* employ their energy and influences in frustrating any movement towards peace, then the evidence given in the following pages should serve to dispel any lingering doubt on these scores. He will, perhaps, have reached that stage of enlightenment when he can join with President Roosevelt in declaring that "this grave menace to the peace of the world [the mad race of armaments] is due in no small way to the uncontrolled activities of the manufacturers of and merchants in engines of destruction".[1]

Throughout the long period during which Bolivia and Paraguay on the one hand and Colombia and Peru on the other were moving along the path to open conflict, and throughout the ensuing hostilities, British and American armament manufacturers poured their weapons of slaughter into the ports and arsenals of these unhappy lands. Never at any stage was a thought given to the use to which these weapons were being put. So long as ready cash was forthcoming, or well-secured credit terms arranged, the traffic continued in an ever-increasing volume, which produced an ever-increasing scale of bloodshed and needless suffering. We have mentioned two of the companies which exploited these South American wars to the full. Others include: E. I. Dupont de Nemours (which sold explosives indiscriminately to Colombia and Peru); the Remington Arms Company (which supplied both protagonists in the Chaco war); Federal Laboratories (which dispensed its favours to all and sundry); and Imperial Chemical Industries (which concentrated mainly on Peru and Paraguay, meeting all the last-named country's cartridge orders).

Some idea of the variety of this traffic can be gained from the findings of a Commission sent out by the League of Nations in 1934 to investigate matters at first hand. The Commission reported that:—

"The armies engaged are using up-to-date material; airplanes, armoured cars, flame-projectors, quick-firing guns

[1] Statement of March 18, 1934.

and auto-rifles. The arms and materials are not manufactured locally but are supplied to the belligerents by American and European countries."

In the House of Commons on May 15, 1934, Mr. Bernays drew the attention of Walter Runciman (then President of the Board of Trade) to the Commission's report, which, he said, clearly implied that there might have been no war at all had these arms not been supplied. He asked the Minister to give an assurance "that the Government will press more strongly than ever for an international agreement to prohibit this hellish traffic". In his reply Mr. Runciman said it was obvious that Britain could not enter into an arrangement of this kind without agreement between the Powers. "I am certainly not prepared to accept any responsibility whatever", he added, "for hostilities between Bolivia and Paraguay".

This Minister, who rejected any responsibility for the bloodshed in the Gran Chaco, had actually licensed the sale to Bolivia of 200 machine-guns, 2,130,550 rounds of ammunition and six tanks, between January, 1932, and March, 1934. In the same period he licensed the sale by I.C.I. of 21,570,000 cartridges to Paraguay.

A plea for the imposition of an embargo on the shipment of arms to Bolivia and Paraguay was first put to the League Council by Mr. de Valera in his report as Chairman of the Council of Three on November 25, 1932. He pointed out that:—

"One of the obstacles to the suspension of hostilities would seem to be the fear on either side of a possible rearmament on the other. As the two members concerned in this dispute are not producers of arms, ammunition, and implements of war, any increase in their belligerent strength depends on consignments from abroad. The Committee therefore feels that the attention of the Governments should be directed to this matter."

To the relief of the armament salesmen, de Valera's suggestion was left hanging in the air, and several months were allowed to elapse before a more definite embargo proposal was submitted.

That they were highly profitable months is shown in a letter written towards the end of 1932 by F. S. Jonas, the Federal Laboratories representative in South America:—

> "The unsettled conditions in South America have been a great thing for me, as I sold a large order of bombs to Brazil and also a fair cartridge order. I also sold very large bomb orders for Colombia, Peru, Ecuador, Bolivia, and now have made up all my losses and am back on my feet. It is an ill wind that does not blow someone some good."[1]

In an earlier letter Jonas informed another colleague that he had "supplied all the bombs and a lot of other military equipment to most of the countries fighting in South America, and if they keep it up much longer I will have no cause to complain".[2]

Jonas had particular cause for satisfaction, inasmuch as there had been a time, in late summer 1932, when it seemed that the dispute between Bolivia and Paraguay would be settled by means which are anathema to arms salesmen—by peaceful negotiation. On August 11, he had penned the following despondent lines to a friend in Buenos Aires:—

> "Your letter addressed to Federal Laboratories with reference to the Paraguay and Bolivia situation was forwarded to me for attention. I immediately took a plane to Washington and visited both the Paraguay and Bolivia Legations. Unfortunately for us, however, it looks as if the trouble they are having is going to be settled amicably."[3]

No doubt the Bolivian and Paraguayan families who lost their men-folk in the subsequent warfare would have found some difficulty in taking Mr. Jonas's view of the situation.

After guerilla skirmishing had lasted for some years, it was in 1932 that active war broke out between the two countries over Chaco. This war was still in progress in September, 1934, and skirmishes and intermittent disputes went on into 1935.

---

[1] Nye Hearings, Part 7, exhibit 665. During the hearings Jonas was described by one of the Senators as "an intellectually honest man".
[2] Ibid., exhibit 740.
[3] Ibid., exhibit 671.

There was also intermittent warfare between Colombia and Peru during 1932 and 1933; an armistice was signed for a year from May 1, 1933, and the final treaty concluded only on May 24, 1934.

All kinds of evidence were produced at the Nye Hearings to illustrate the variety of methods and representatives used by the armament firms in the South American republics. Not the least picturesque was the case of the missionary brother of John W. Young, President of Federal Laboratories. After being a missionary for some twelve years in Ecuador, he wrote to his brother, with whom he seemed to have been in frequent pious contact, a letter from which the following are extracts :—

"My dear John,

Since writing you last we have been in our Indian station in Agato, Otavalo. We had a week of joyful simple life. Our visit was a blessing to us and we have reason to believe it was also a blessing to Miss Brown and Miss Robel, the two brave girls stationed there. Six or eight Indians showed a desire to follow the Lord and we prayed with them. Some of them had made previous beginnings but had been pulled down by sin. Indian work needs a great deal of prayer.

"Yesterday I saw the Minister of War again and made arrangements to demonstrate today. The Minister, two generals, the head of the Police of Quito and a number of officers and soldiers were present. I used the 'Billy' first but I am sorry to say it did not prove a success. I shot it at two soldiers but they were able to stand the gas and get me. I then shot the grenade in a room and asked the men to go in. This was a real success and helped to gain what I had lost through the failure of the Billie.

"Colonel Santor happened to be here on a visit and he witnessed the demonstration. I found out through his conversation with the Minister that he, it seemed, secured some gas grenades (larger than yours and black) through the American brewer, Yoder. This is no doubt the reason he has been putting me off. It is more than likely that he got something out of it.

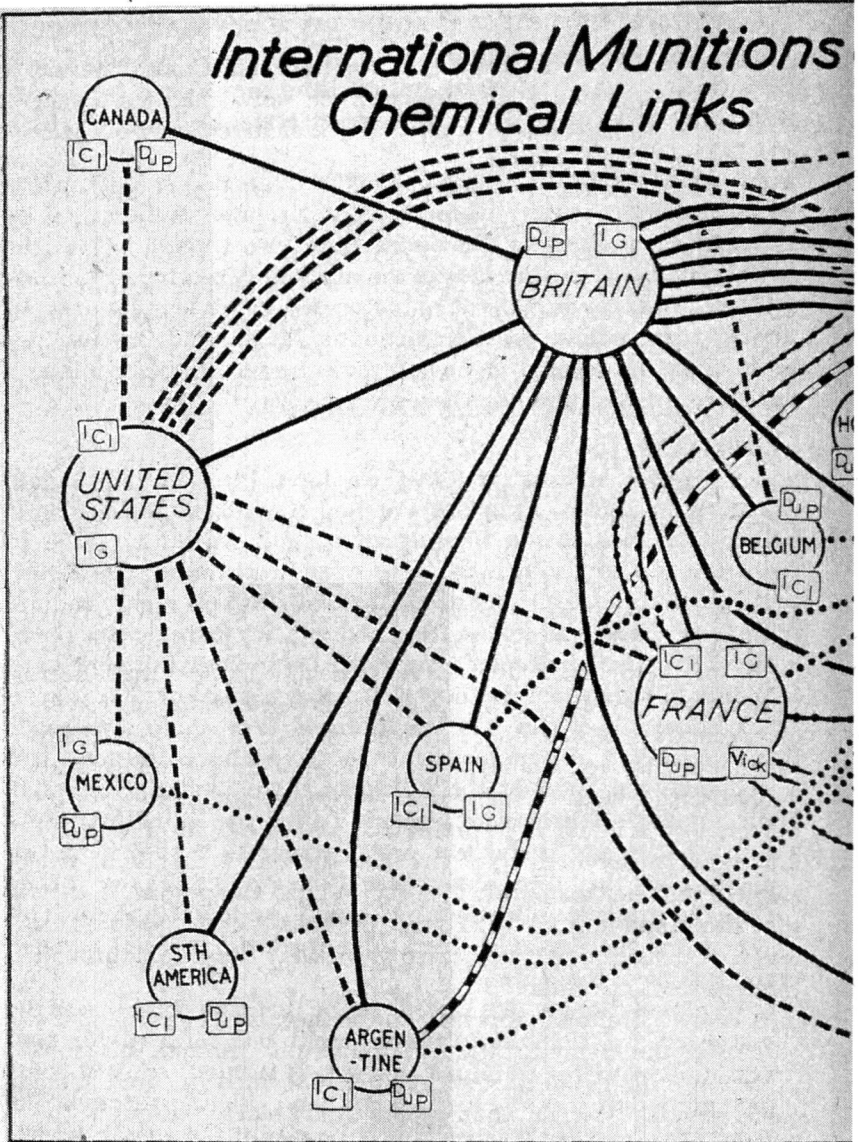

International Munitions
Chemical Links

CANADA
ICI — DuP

BRITAIN
DuP IG

UNITED
STATES
ICI
IG

HO
DuP

BELGIUM
DuP
ICI

FRANCE
ICI IG
DuP Vick

MEXICO
IG
DuP

SPAIN
ICI — IG

STH
AMERICA
ICI — DuP

ARGEN
-TINE
ICI — DuP

This chart is based on data published by the Nye Committee
world-wars, and does not,

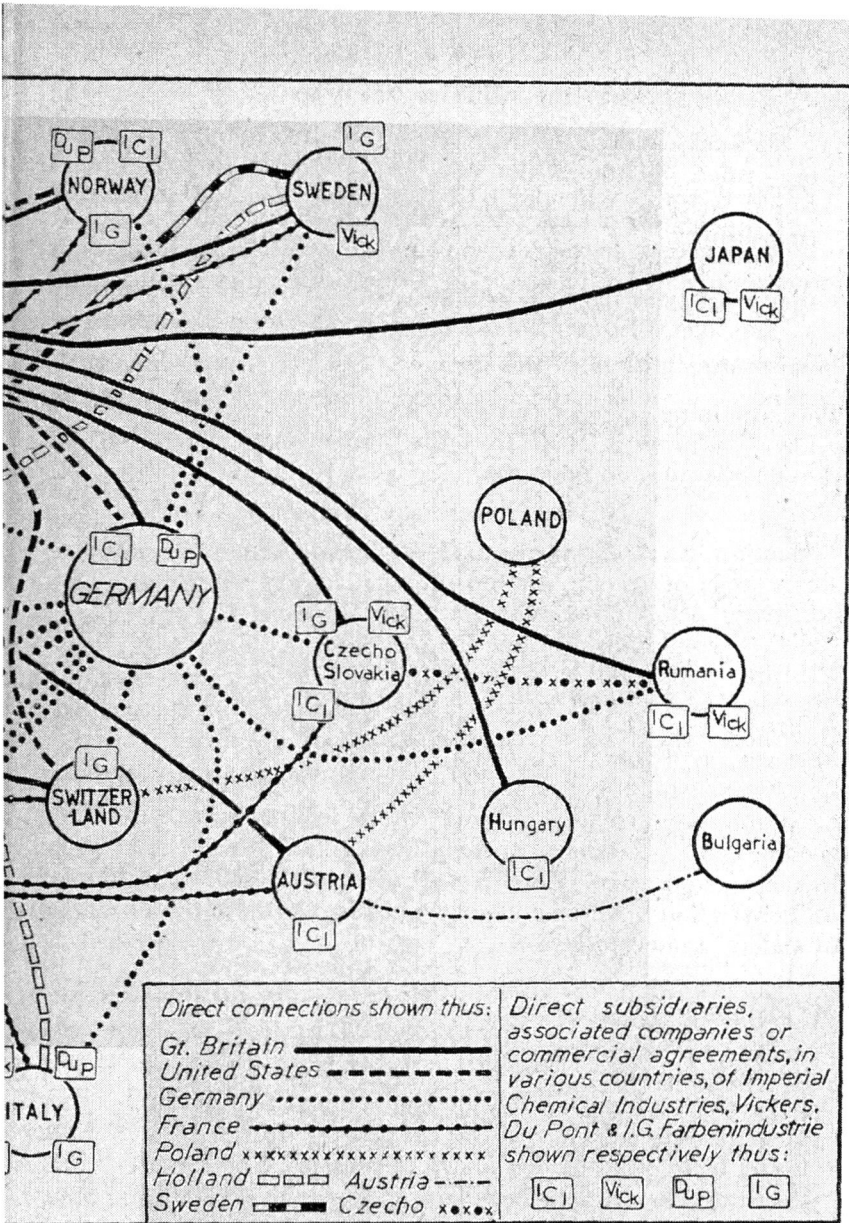

Direct connections shown thus:

Gt. Britain ——————
United States – – – – –
Germany ••••••••••••••
France ••–••–••–••–••–••
Poland xxxxxxxxxxxxxxxxxxxx
Holland ▭▭▭   Austria –··–··–
Sweden ▰▱▰▱   Czecho x•x•x

Direct subsidiaries, associated companies or commercial agreements, in various countries, of Imperial Chemical Industries, Vickers, Du Pont & I.G. Farbenindustrie shown respectively thus:

| ICI | Vick | DuP | IG |

Map labels: NORWAY, SWEDEN, JAPAN, GERMANY, POLAND, Czecho Slovakia, Rumania, SWITZER-LAND, Hungary, Bulgaria, AUSTRIA, ITALY

It shows the ramifications of the armament cartels between the two
, apply to the present day.

"Before leaving, the Minister asked me to give him the best price on 100 Billies and 200 grenades. I told him I would write to you and have you send him quotations and terms direct.

". . . I have a letter from the Reed boys telling me that they are getting in touch with you. It may be best to have them as your agents from now on but I don't think they should come in for any of this order, as I . . ."[1]

The remaining page of this gem was lost and not produced in evidence, but it is clear that the "missionary" was after his commission, and no nonsense.

No Peace for the Wicked

Mention has already been made of Mr. de Valera's suggestion late in 1932 of an embargo on shipment of arms to Bolivia and Paraguay. Although consideration of the matter was suspended, there was some talk on these lines in the early months of 1933. A British proposal for an embargo in February was delayed, however, and finally nothing was done, as "it was hoped that there would be an early cessation of hostilities". In the meantime the armament "boys" were feeling quite sure that, according to precedent, nothing would be done to stop their lucrative commerce. Here is the view of a representative of du Pont in South America, as expressed in a letter to the President of Federal Laboratories :—

"My dear John,

". . . I spent a very quiet but very pleasant Christmas despite the rotten weather. Regarding the attempts of Mr. Hoover and the cooky pushers in the State Department to effect embargoes on munitions sent out of the country—I do not believe there is the least occasion for alarm at present. The President and the State Department both lack authority to do anything now, and in the spirit that Congress is in and with the large amount

[1] Nye Hearings, Part 7, exhibit 747.

of oral business ahead I feel quite sure that no further authority will be granted."[1]

Mr. Monaghan, Manager of the Foreign Department for Remington, wrote at about the same time, January 4, 1933, to their agent in Chile, Mr. J. H. Spencer. After some details about current business, he went on:—

"About the agitation for an embargo on arms and ammunition from the United States, you can well appreciate when this first reached our ears from Washington, *we immediately got busy*, and we are thoroughly satisfied from the reports that came back to us there will be no embargo from this country. From what we hear the idea originated with the State Department, but is not receiving any serious consideration in Congress or by the President. We reached some mighty high officials in the Government and feel confident nothing will prevent the execution of any business we can get.

"There is not a chance of any legislation going through without our knowing of it being started, and the steps we have taken will, we feel sure, enable us to get the opportunity to fully present our arguments which will kill any of *these crazy ideas*."[2]

"Getting busy" meant that the armament companies set to and pulled every string they could to impede the avowed aims of their Governments to establish some sort of arrangement whereby the shipping of arms to these non-producing countries could be stopped. Mr. Goss, President of the Lake Erie Chemical Company, did not hesitate, as is shown in this extract from a letter he wrote on January 10, 1933:—

"In regard to the telegram you sent me yesterday regarding the arms embargo bill, the most powerful lobby in Washington is that conducted by the American Legion. Immediately upon receipt of your wire, I had a telegram sent to Traylor, who is head of the American Legion lobby, by the Ohio State

[1] Nye Hearings, Part 5, exhibit 482.
[2] *Ibid.*, Part 10, exhibit 907.

Commander of the American Legion and the national commander of the '40 and 8', which has probably a million members, requesting that every ounce of pressure be brought to bear to stop any such foolish action . . ."[1]

On February 8 of the same year, Mr. C. W. Webster, sales representative of Latin-American Curtiss-Wright products, wrote to Captain C. K. Travis, the company's representative in Peru :—

". . . In my opinion the real activity is just beginning, not only in the Chaco but around Leticia as well. National pride and stubbornness will not permit these countries to quit until they blow up through absolute bankruptcy, and while the show is going on, it is our job as distributors of munitions to get our share. . . . I am still of the opinion that before these two 'comic opera wars' are finished in the north and south that practically all of South America will be involved—so watch your step and play your cards carefully."[2]

Mr. C. W. Webster's rather macabre sense of comedy was not, at that time, being shared by the rest of the world. While these letters were being written, the nations were being asked to consider the appeal made by Mr. Eden to their accredited representatives on the League of Nations to play their cards cleanly for the open game of peace. Here are some of the ways Mr. Webster was playing his own cards :—

I

Letter to Mr. J. Van Wagner, Chile. March 30, 1933.

". . . Again please remember to refrain in all of your letters sent to this office from mentioning the name of Orsini. You can always refer to him as 'Jones'. Also do not converse with anyone regarding sale of machines or equipment going to other countries or any transactions concerning them. As mentioned in my previous letter, conditions are becoming

[1] Nye Hearings, Part 8, exhibit 777.
[2] *Ibid.*, Part 4, exhibit 348.

very acute and I do not wish our files to contain anything with a bearing on this business. You can always send any necessary letters to my home and thereby keep them out of our files. . . .

"Another matter which I wish you would take up immediately and possibly through Dias Lira is the question involving the possible manufacture in the Santiago plant of airplanes intended for other.South American countries. This is in view of a possible embargo on the part of the League of Nations and United States Government."[1]

II

Letter to Mr. Lawrence Leon, Argentina. February 10, 1933 (after suggesting that Mr. Leon should contact some Government officials in Paraguay).

"It seems to me that the Bolivia–Paraguay trouble has not yet reached its peak and the conditions instead of becoming better are gradually getting worse. If such is the case, it will be absolutely necessary for Paraguay to find the money for the purchase of aircraft and other munitions. If we are able to sell them anything, we will have to work very carefully and quietly, and possibly work through you, as an individual, as the Bolivian Government would naturally raise 'merry hell' if they believed that we were dealing with their enemies."[2]

III

Letter to Mr. E. J. Faucett, Peru. February 9, 1933.

". . . Please remember that no spare engines have yet been purchased for the Hawks, so please bring a little pressure to bear on the Air Corps officials and on Mr. Fardo, and see if this business cannot be concluded in the near future. For your confidential information, you might diplomatically inform interested parties that your neighbour to the extreme north is still purchasing in large quantities. Do not overlook such items as bombs, ammunition, machine guns, equipment, etc."[3]

[1] Nye Hearings, Part 4, exhibit 364.
[2] *Ibid.*, exhibit 360.
[3] Nye Hearings, Part 4, exhibit 355.

Similar designs, no doubt, prompted the negotiations by the Lake Erie Chemical Company to build, equip and staff with experts a poison-gas plant in Colombia. Their catalogue outlines the uses to which this desirable product could be put, and these arguments were used freely to all Governments whom they could interest with their usual sales approaches:—

Examples: *Catalogue of the United States Ordnance Engineers, Inc.*

"Mustard gas is the ideal defense agent. It is very persistent, lasting in an area under some conditions as long as a week. It is possible with mustard gas to prohibit territory to advancing land forces, whether infantry, cavalry, or tanks, with far less expenditures of either life or money than by any other known means. . . .

"Mustard gas is also tactically valuable for producing casualties in advance of the time of an attack, or for producing casualties in and isolating strong points which may be avoided during attack. . . .

"Phosgene is the most practical and economical gas for the production of quick death. While mustard-gas casualties are a long time in hospital, sometimes several months, there is nothing about them, immediately after being gassed, to inspire terror in other troops. With phosgene, however, if heavily gassed, men will be dropping dead like flies within a few hours."[1]

And Lake Erie Chemical Company would be only too pleased to advise, draw up plans and supply all necessary materials and exports for the production of the gases they were here advertising in their catalogue, and would naturally draw good dividends at the job, whether men were "dropping dead like flies" or not.

In their letters to one another, many of the Merchants of

[1] Nye Hearings, Part 8, pp. 2009, 2010. It should be noted that the use of poison gas was prohibited by the Geneva Gas Protocol of 1925, to which most of the principal Powers of the world subscribed.

Death reveal that they at least are not bothered by sentimental prejudices such as patriotism, any more than they are with right or wrong, or even public honesty, or loyalty to the declared policies of their Governments, or international agreements. Indiscriminate internationalism in business is a first principle with them, however reprehensible it is in their eyes in the world of politics. This paragraph from a long letter sent by an agent in Mexico to the Curtiss-Wright Corporation in August, 1933, gives a clear view of their purpose :—

". . . Watson, Phillips and Co. is the oldest British firm in Mexico, having been in business over a hundred years. They are very active and the financial rating is very high. I looked up two other firms but was not as favourably impressed. We need not fear their being partial toward British products, they have been too long in this country and will favour whoever gives them a better deal. They have some American employees, use only American cars and only recently could have sold a British plane to the British Chargé d'Affaires but preferred to sell him an American ship instead."[1]

But all good things must draw to an end sometime, and, to the undisguised dismay of the arms traffickers, there were signs that one or two of the parties engaged in fighting in South America, as well as one or two other States not actually at war, were contemplating negotiations for a cessation of hostilities. One of the agents whom we have met before, Mr. J. Van Wagner, writes to Mr. Webster again in a quaint turn of phrase about this threat to their prosperity :—

". . . With the present action taken by the Chilean Foreign Minister to foment peace in South America, he cannot possibly give his consent to allow war material to leave Chile, especially to a country engaged in warfare. Consequently we are stuck in the mud."[2]

. Mr. Webster, as one would expect, was alarmed at the thought of peace anywhere, but especially when they were doing such

[1] Nye Hearings, Part 4, exhibit 333.
[2] *Ibid.*, exhibit 363.

good business in death-materials in South America itself. He writes to Captain Travis in haste when the end looks near:—

". . . If Webster and Ashton are able to work fast enough they may be able to get the additional nine or sixteen planes closed before the war ends. The consul general in New York seems to feel quite certain that the mess will be cleaned up within a month. I certainly hope we will be able to get some more business before this happens."[1]

Captain Travis was of the same mind, and did not intend to miss any chance of mulcting the warring States; in a letter replying to Webster he cynically remarks:—

". . . we must not neglect Bolivia; they are our best customers at the present time. A small country but they have come across with nearly half a million dollars in the past year and are good for quite a bit more if the war lasts."[2]

And about a month later Webster is writing from Bolivia (where he went himself to make sure of getting orders) to New York to show that he had fully grasped the importance of the fact that Bolivia would "be good for a bit more":—

". . . Am writing this letter at midnight—just returned from dinner after a late session with Lopez and the Minister of War. . . . The Government wishes to acquire 10 large bombing planes and it is a choice between Junker and ourselves.

"The financial end of the job is naturally all important. Lopez wishes to do a deal with us for the bombers and probably other material which will run possibly to between $800,000 and $1,000,000. . . .

"Hope we can come to some sort of agreement as there is plenty of business here. Lopez told me tonight frankly and confidentially that Bolivia had no intention of making peace until they got what they were after and, if necessary, the entire Patino company could back their stand."[3]

Mr. Webster had some time before considered that Bolivia

---

[1] Nye Hearings, Part 4, exhibit 342.
[2] *Ibid.*, exhibit 343.   [3] *Ibid.*, exhibit 349.

would be able to find funds for the purchase of munitions, either from Standard Oil, who have large concessions there (actually in the Chaco district), or from the Patino company, mentioned in the above letter, which is a large tin-mining company in Bolivia.

In December, 1933, a conference was held in Rio de Janeiro with the aim of bringing the Chaco hostilities to an end. Wrote a Colombian agent to the vice-president of the Curtiss-Wright Export Corporation:—

". . . it is evident that efforts to convince the Government of the need and advisability of making immediate additions to our air force have been effective. The likelihood of failure of the Rio Conference has aided us considerably in this endeavour."[1]

In the whole of the Nye hearings there is only one instance of armament manufacturers or salesmen recognizing the ethical undesirability of their activities, and this is in a letter from Mr. Jonas to Mr. Owen Shannon of the Curtiss-Wright Aviation Corporation:—

"MY DEAR OWEN,

Thanks very much for your most amusing Christmas card, which gave me a laugh, and Lord knows we need one these days.

"The Paraguay and Bolivia fracas appears to be coming to a termination, so business from that end is probably finished. We certainly are in one hell of a business, where a fellow has to wish for trouble so as to make a living, the only consolation being however that if we don't get the business someone else will. It would be a terrible state of affairs if my conscience started to bother me now."[2]

When the inevitable lull came, the arms agents were still ceaselessly plotting for situations and circumstances to favour their traffic. Mr. Webster had the idea that the appointment of one of their own nominees as a Peruvian Government official would help their sales:—

[1] Nye Hearings, Part 4, exhibit 339. [2] *Ibid.*, exhibit 338.

". . . I am sorry that Melgar did not take over the job of Inspector General of Aviation of Peru, but, possibly, as military attaché in Chile he can still be of considerable service. If the Government intends to put in a foreigner, and, possibly, an American, in charge of aviation, who do they have in mind? I certainly hope that Grove does not go back to Peru. Why not apply for the job yourself and see if we cannot work out a situation whereby we could all profit by it."[1]

The scramble for orders still went on during the armistice periods, the Governments, with the willing help of the arms firms, buying heavily towards the end of the term in preparation for the possible resumption of warfare. An agent, Mr. Miranda, wrote to the company he represented:—

"As you know, the armistice with Peru comes to an end in about 60 days; both Peru and Colombia are making great preparations and a big time is expected by all.

"It being impossible to sell both to Peru and Colombia, because one would not buy from you if the other one did, we have chosen Colombia, first and foremost because they have money (which Peru has very little of), and, then, because of the fact that our connections in official circles in Colombia are just made to order. . . .

"Aside from that, the writer's brother is down in Bogota, where we are negotiating sales of war material running into several millions of dollars."[2]

Mr. Miranda was, however, mistaken when he thought they could not sell to both parties, for this was done regularly by as many of the firms as could manage to do so with impunity. One of his fellow-agents was at the same period writing to his firm in North America asking them to be more careful in their dealings, as he was in danger of "seeing the inside of jail" for selling to the other side!

[1] Nye Hearings, Part 4, exhibit 316.
[2] *Ibid.*, Part 3, exhibit 245.

PAX BRITANNICA

Even when an embargo was passed through Congress in May, 1934, there were holes in it which allowed the armaments firms to wriggle through. Mr. Cordell Hull, after representations had been made, pronounced that the embargo did not apply to orders entered into and partly paid by the Governments before the date of its enactment. That the Merchants of Death were well prepared to exploit such a loophole can be judged from this letter written by Mr. Huber, sales agent for U.S. Ordnance Engineers, to Colonel Goss, President of Lake Erie Chemical Company. The date is May 11, 1934, or one week only before the embargo was introduced into Congress :—

"DEAR COLONEL,

"According to papers of this morning, it seems as though the League of Nations is going to eliminate South American bomb business. With your permission, I will send a cable to Mayrink Veiga, or you could send it directly, suggesting that they place the bomb order with us immediately *and ante-dating the contract* so that we could be in a position to fill the order, because it is altogether possible that any move on the part of the League of Nations would not hinder existing contracts."[1]

After the embargo had been imposed, on July 13, Mr. Huber wrote to his firm about various business and reported on what he had heard concerning a rival firm's practice :—

". . . The grapevine also reports that the Bolivian order was increased to $3,000,000 from an original order of $241,000 in order to get round the embargo, as Secretary Hull finally ruled that any contracts made prior to May 28 were not affected by the embargo. . . ."[2]

But even if it was not possible to arrange things in this way, there remained the wholly satisfactory method, used regularly and freely in most parts of the world by the armaments international, of falsely labelling shipments. The evidence of Mr.

[1] Nye Hearings, Part 8, exhibit 764. (Our italics.)
[2] *Ibid.*, exhibit 765.

Hamilton, Deputy Collector of Customs in the Port of New York, made it quite clear that this was really a simple procedure which would generally pass unquestioned :—

"*Senator Clark*: And by misbranding the goods, in violation of the law in the case of an embargo, that can be accomplished and there is nothing to be done about it?

"*Mr. Hamilton*: Nothing to prevent them, unless the activities of the steamship companies do it, and, of course, they are looking to get the proper freight rate."

At the same time as these moves were taking place in the United States, the Prime Minister and others were having to answer questions in the House of Commons on the issue of the proposed embargo of armaments shipments to Bolivia and Paraguay. Replying to Mr. Vyvyan Adams on May 16, Mr. Baldwin said, in effect, that the proposal had really been delayed by the statement of the Government of the United States that "they were unable to impose an embargo until the necessary legislation had been passed by Congress, and no such legislation had been passed". In making this reply Mr. Baldwin was throwing the responsibility for failure on to the American Government. On May 29, the Prime Minister said that the Government agreed "in principle" to the proposal to impose the embargo on Bolivia and Paraguay, but in fact no embargo was imposed until five months later. In the meantime orders which might have gone to the American manufacturers were going to I.C.I., which, of course, was not covered by the U.S. embargo. The du Pont agent was a joint agent with I.C.I. and was able to switch orders to I.C.I. when the American embargo came into force. Thus, on page 1119 of the Nye Hearings, Part 5, we read :—

"*Senator Vandenberg*: Yet Mr. Bates, writing in the name of your company, scrupulously observes that prescription (the recent embargo); but while he does that with his right hand, his left hand is notifying the I.C.I. that some munitions orders are awaiting in Bolivia and Paraguay."

Later in the hearing it came out that in any case there was an agreement that du Pont paid the entire salary of the agent,

Mr. Bates, and that they got a commission on *all sales*, both for themselves and for I.C.I.; thus they were able to respect the letter of the embargo and ignore its spirit with no loss to themselves.

In the House of Commons on June 4, 1934, Sir John Simon confirmed that the U.S. President had on May 28 issued a proclamation forbidding the sale *within the U.S.A.* of arms and munitions to either Bolivia or Paraguay. As far as he knew, the proclamation did not prohibit the sale of arms to a third person outside the U.S. who re-sold to either belligerent. Only a few weeks earlier, in May, when the Council of the League of Nations were at a critical point in their negotiations for the prevention of war between Colombia and Peru, *Vickers sold two destroyers to Colombia* and the First Lord of the Admiralty gave permission for 100 British ex-officers and ratings to assist Colombia in manning these vessels.

The *News Chronicle*, on May 16, 1934, reported that:—

"The quarrel between Colombia and Peru, which had almost been settled by the League, shows signs of breaking out again because these countries have once more acquired the means to fight".

Practical political moves were very difficult to initiate. Even when Mr. Ramsay MacDonald, who had been an ardent opponent of war at one period of his life and had long been active in exposing the nefarious work of the Merchants of Death, was Prime Minister, he stone-walled. Asked by Mr. Mander if he would consider the advisability of appointing a special committee to investigate the charges made that private armament interests had been responsible for fomenting discord between nations with a view to their own financial profit, the Prime Minister said he was "not aware that any such charge had been formulated by anyone in a manner sufficiently concrete and/or substantiated to warrant or bear examination". Compare this disingenuous statement with the letter sent out in July 1934 by Federal Laboratories to all its agents:—

"We take keen delight in advising you that the first six months of 1934 has been the most successful period in the history of our company. Total sales up to June 30 are three times as great as those for any single preceding year. A very gratifying feature of this excellent sales record is the important part that has been played by the export part of our business. To those of you who have contributed to this marvelous record we extend our sincere appreciation and congratulations. We know it has taken a lot of hard work to get this business, but it has paid dividends.

"With conditions of unrest as they are today throughout the world, you have a real opportunity before you if you will only get back of this thing and push the Federal program."[1]

The Disarmament Conference was sitting during perhaps the most active period of these operations, with the declared aim of bringing about an all-round reduction in armaments. The only *unilateral* actions taken were the introduction of the "licence" system in Britain for the export of arms and the final U.S. embargo. The British licence regulations were, of course, full of holes: licences applied only to exports from the United Kingdom—thus firms with foreign plants (Vickers and I.C.I., for instance) were not subject to licence in that respect; they did not cover the export of planes; they did not cover the export of chemical substances (such as those used for gas); information as to the character of the export and the place of destination was published only after the arms had left United Kingdom ports, and, since no names were demanded, was quite inadequate.

The actual discussions on the suggestion of an embargo were not begun until 1933, and we have seen in this chapter something of the contribution made towards their success by the armaments manufacturers in their day-to-day business. It was obviously ridiculous to discuss a Bolivia, or Colombia, or Paraguay embargo in 1933 when British and American statistics show that the South American belligerents had *already been fully equipped* by the Merchants of Death long before any effective control on the traffic could be imposed. It was not until October 31, 1934, that Sir John Simon announced in the House of Commons that the embargo had "at last been put into operation".

[1] Nye Hearings, Part 7, exhibit 714.

CHAPTER V

TOKYO CUSTOMER

"The Japanese murderers were without a sword. America gave them the sword."

General Li Chung-jen, the victor of Taierhchwang.[1]

Sir Philip Gibbs: "Those specialities, whatever they may have been, were for the invasion, no doubt, of Manchukuo?"
Sir Harry McGowan: "Yes."
Sir Philip Gibbs: "And at the very same time you were supplying the Chinese with the same materials of war in order to repel that invasion?"
Sir Harry McGowan: "Yes."

Royal Commission hearings.

". . . But to have to stand by while even the very poor are having their last possession taken from them—their last bit of bedding (and it is freezing weather), the poor ricksha man his ricksha; while thousands of disarmed soldiers who had sought sanctuary with you, together with many hundreds of innocent civilians, are taken out before your eyes to be shot or used for bayonet practice, and you have to listen to the sound of the guns that are killing them; while a thousand women kneel before you crying hysterically, begging you to save them from the beasts that are preying on them . . . this is a hell I had never before envisaged. Robbery, murder, rape continue unabated. A rough estimate would be at least a thousand women raped last night and during the day. One poor woman was raped thirty-seven times. Another had her five months' infant deliberately smothered by the brute to stop its crying while he raped her. Resistance means the bayonet . . ."

THERE ARE many pages of such harrowing descriptions of war in the Far East in Mr. H. J. Timperley's book *What War Means*. But it was not until 1938 that this book was published, and China had been the happy hunting-ground of the Merchants of Death for many years before the people of Britain and America were given a real view of the sufferings and horrors described by this eye-witness. The people of China, like the people of Mr. Chamberlain's Czechoslovakia, "live very far away", and it is an unfortunate fact that, in the piping days of peace, the British people took very little interest in the happenings with which they were not directly concerned. Some there were, in that period, who publicly deplored the activities of those armament combines which were exploiting the Far Eastern situation for their own profit, but they were distressingly few, and had next to no success. Everything that is included in this chapter must be read with this awful picture always in mind: of a war-devastated country with a

[1] *Battle Hymn of China*, Agnes Smedley (Gollancz).

population of millions of miserable and illiterate people swept up in all sorts of major and minor wars, petty quarrels and disputes, and massacred, pillaged and savaged by local and national tyrants for more than twenty years.

For this length of time, armed bands, some large enough to be called armies, were roaming about the land of China, extorting taxes and tribute from the people wherever they went, massacring and robbing where they found resistance, and fighting with one another for local supremacy. *Their armies were equipped with European weapons, and their representatives and officers came to Europe to visit its great armament firms—Creusot, Vickers, Krupps—and to place orders for the latest types of weapons.* As their conquests grew, their financial commitments increased correspondingly, and the munitions they were obliged to buy for their protection had to be paid for with ever-increasing taxation of the peasants whose lands they had overrun.

The attitude of the leaders of the various large combines which were arming the different factions in China can be seen from the interrogation of Sir Harry McGowan (now Lord McGowan) by the Royal Commission in 1935. Here are one or two questions and answers extracted from the report:—

"2866. *Sir Philip Gibbs:* May I read it [a Nye exhibit] again? 'I.C.I. are trying to solve the Far Eastern question to the best of their ability.' Does that mean you were trying to create peace in the Far East?

"*Sir Harry McGowan:* Surely not. It is not our job to create peace.

"2845. *Sir Philip Gibbs:* May I ask you whether there was any feeling of delicacy in your mind as to, perhaps, the impropriety or, at any rate, the inadvisability of selling military propellants and explosives to the Chinese Government when in other parts of China you were selling things for the purpose of agriculture and so forth?

"*Sir Harry McGowan:* No. I have no delicacy of feeling in the matter at all.

"*Sir Philip Gibbs:* Not the slightest?

"*Sir Harry McGowan:* No."

Generally one can say that these emperors of the Bloody
International had one policy: to sell quite indiscriminately to all
comers at the best prices they could obtain for their deadly wares.
It was immaterial to them which side was generally agreed to be
the aggressor in a particular conflict; they had arms enough to
sell to the condemned as well as to the pitied, and they were well
content. And of course their sales to one party could only fan the
flame and increase the anxiety of the others. The results are
written in the blood of the peasants of the Chinese provinces
whom the various war-lords starved or whipped into their armies
during the ebb and flow of constant internecine warfare, from
the time of the Great War until the final terror of Japanese
aggression in Manchuria. Here is Hallett Abend's picture of
those years in *Tortured China*:—

". . . a rabble of ignorant armed men about 2,500,000
strong, any unit of which will fight for any faction or any cause
at the bidding of any commander who, by hook or crook, can
raise enough money to feed and clothe them and occasionally
give them a few silver coins.

"Dredge most of these commanders from the depths of society,
put into the hands of these ignorant but crafty, rapacious,
ambitious and unscrupulous commanders the power of life and
death over the populations of the regions they control, imagine
the unarmed populations helpless and cowed to the point of
meekly enduring the confiscations, duplicated taxes, corrupt
or craven magistrates.

". . . one must further imagine nearly one-tenth of the
population living perpetually below the line of proper nourish-
ment; one must envision annual droughts and floods affecting
large areas, and vast inaccessible districts in which millions of
human beings have killed and eaten all the livestock and even
the dogs, and now subsist largely upon roots and grasses, leaves
and the bark of trees.

". . . at Nanking, on the Yangtsze, a body of men trying
to govern this enormous area of affliction. Picture this Government being continually forced to wage one war after another
in order even to continue a precarious existence. Vision about

D

nineteen-twentieths of this Government's revenues being
expended for military purposes and for interest on foreign
loans."

There was a terrible shambles of human society and complete
social and moral chaos, a source of constant horror and pity in
the better-informed circles of the outside world—and a happy
hunting-ground for the agents of the munitions and powder
companies in the West who worked on the comfortable principle
that it was "not their job to create peace".

Here is Lord McGowan again to throw more light on the
mental attitude of the armament manufacturer in his extensive
business with the Far Eastern war-mongers. After admitting that
I.C.I. supplied Japan with certain specialities (some of which
were used in the manufacture of poison gas) and that this material
was for use in the invasion of Manchuria, Sir Harry was brought
to admitting that he would continue to sell such material unless
stopped by the Government—even though their customer had
been publicly declared the aggressor. (Chemical shipments to
Japan over the period 1931–1933 included: 1 ton of chlorine;
2,069 tons of ammonium nitrate; and 34 tons of ethylene glycol.
All can be used in the production of poison gas.)

The Japanese invaded Manchuria in 1931, thereby violating
two treaties to which Britain was a party, the Kellogg Pact and
the Nine-Power Treaty. Yet at the time of the attack on Manchuria the British Government refused to join with the U.S.
Government in a protest to Japan. At a League meeting in 1932,
Lord Lytton's Commission of Inquiry reported that Japan was
the aggressor. But Sir John Simon's speech was sufficient to sway
the meeting in Japan's favour. As Mr. Matsuoko said to a group
of newspaper men in the lobby after the session: "What I have
been trying to say in my bad English for the last ten days, Sir
John Simon has said in his excellent English in half an hour"!
Soon afterwards, Matsuoka trotted off to England, where,
naturally enough, he became the honoured guest of Metropolitan-
Vickers, and was taken on a tour of their works and those of I.C.I.

We have recorded earlier that Sir John Simon held shares in
the I.C.I. His action in selling them as soon as his attention was

drawn to the matter removes any suggestion that he was animated by personal interests when he supported Japan's case at the League. Nevertheless, the general principle that those who direct national policy should not be associated with industrial concerns closely related to war remains valid. Mr. W. Arnold-Forster expressed it to the Royal Commission when he said that "it cannot be healthy for the repute of a Government if it is known that Cabinet Ministers may be in a position to benefit personally, however slightly, from the breakdown of disarmament negotiations and from the placing of orders with armament firms by their colleagues who speak for the fighting services. . . . I venture to suggest that there are objections to a system in which two interests, the one public and the other private, may be so closely intertwined."

No doubt Matsuoka's English hosts were as distressed as their American counterparts at the outbreak of war between their old customers China and Japan. This concern was reflected in a letter written by one du Pont official to another and produced at the Nye Hearings.

"Please advise what steps have been taken to secure military sales business in the unhappy event of hostilities between China and Japan." (F. W. Pickard, Vice-President of du Pont.)

The British agents were as concerned, and as busy, for similar reasons—I.C.I. (Metals), Ltd., manufacturing most of the munitions for Japan during 1932. In that year the Board of Trade issued forty-two export licences for the shipment of war materials to Japan and thirty-one for China. Under those permits Japan received 5,361,450 cartridges, ten howitzers or mortars, 740 machine-guns and £160,000 worth of old military equipment. *This was the year of the Disarmament Conference!* Other members of the Government holding shares in I.C.I. were Mr. Neville and Mr. Austen Chamberlain.

Largely as the result of pressure of public opinion, the British Government decided, in February, 1933, to grant no new licences outside the then existing contracts for arms exports to the belligerent countries. This embargo had previously been discussed in the

United States, individually by the producing countries (mainly France and Great Britain) and also collectively at Geneva. On March 9, Mr. Baldwin was asked whether the embargo would affect the Air Ministry licences of 1932 granted for the manufacture of aircraft in Japan. He replied that it did "not affect the manufacture of aircraft in Japan". This meant that the British firms which had associated factories in Japan were virtually unaffected by the embargo. As no similar action was taken by the other Powers, the British embargo was soon withdrawn. According to official returns—which are always far from giving an accurate picture of such matters—British armament exports to Japan rose from £98,200 in 1929 to £230,000 in 1932. The figures for exports to China were £16,700 for 1930 and £7,300 for 1932! Thus, during the critical years of Japanese aggression the British armament firms gave their strongest support to the aggressor.

Rather surprisingly, the Chinese figure rose to £223,500 for 1933, but we must remember that that year saw the beginning of the counter-revolution by Chiang Kai-Shek and his assault on the established and successful Chinese soviet republics. Would it be reading too much into these figures to suggest that the British armament firms had developed a marked preference for the forces of reaction in China? On March 29, 1933, the President of the Board of Trade, Dr. Burgin, stated that during the eighteen months ended February, 1933, the total declared value of the domestic value of ordnance and high explosive from the United Kingdom to China and Japan amounted to £51,816 and £399,653 respectively. Small wonder, if anything comparable was going on between the other producing Powers and the belligerents, that the aggressor was so consistently victorious.

Though Japan has always been recognized as America's most dangerous enemy, she has also been one of America's best customers for the purchase of war material. During the Nye hearings it was revealed that very large supplies of armaments and war materials were going from the U.S. to Japan. America was always opposed to the growth of Japan as a naval Power in the Pacific, but we find that our old friend the Electric Boat Company built quite a number of submarines for Japan in the years 1931–1934. Mr. Tupper was Chief of the Division of Foreign Trade Statistics, U.S. Bureau of Foreign and Domestic Commerce, and appeared before the Nye Committee with the following information among his evidence:—

"Our exports of bar lead to Japan account for almost all o our exports of bar lead. In 1932 we had a total export of bar lead to all countries of 46,774,658 pounds avoirdupois. In that year roughly 40 millions of those pounds went to Japan. . . . In 1933 a similar condition existed. Our total exports were in excess of 45 million pounds and our exports to Japan were in excess of 42 million pounds."

Mr. Tupper also disclosed that "exports of scrap-iron and steel to Japan in 1933 represent an increase over 1929 of 163%". Lockheed planes of the very latest type were supplied to Japan by the American Armament Corporation, as shown by the President of the Corporation when he admitted at the Nye hearing that "the Japanese Imperial Navy is now equipped with the latest model Lockheed plane". Senator Bone of the investigating committee here inserted a comment which has pungent meaning to us reading it after Pearl Harbour:—

. "Out on the Pacific Coast . . . we are interested in this because we are being told . . . that the Japanese are preparing to fly the Great Circle route and bomb our Puget Sound cities. I am a bit curious to know about the type of plane that is going to blow me off the earth."

. While Japan bought large quantities of finished war material from British and American companies, this is by no means all the story. Most of the companies had also taken care to establish financial interests in Japan. Mitsui and Co., as well as being one of the most important export markets for I.C.I., was linked with them through the Nippon Steel Works, which was controlled by Vickers. I.C.I. also controlled Brunner-Mond (Japan), a subsidiary sales company. At the Nye hearings it was revealed that another company, Mitsubishu, was under licence to Vickers to use the latter's patents for armaments; and here we come upon one of the most important forms of aid in the building up of the mighty power of Japan—the granting of patent rights which enabled her to produce specialized armaments in' domestic factories. Needless to say, the western armament firms drew handsome royalties on these patent licences. No pains were spared to see that the Japanese industry was placed on a good footing; numbers of experts were sent over by the British and American firms to supervise the erection and operation of plant and constant touch was maintained by both sides.

THE ARSENAL OF DEMOCRACY

During the House of Commons debate on the private manufacture and trade in arms, Sir John Simon declared with some heat that "some critics seemed to think that it was quite right for private manufacturers to export arms to China but quite wrong to export them to Japan". Subsequent events have shown that the critics who annoyed Sir John Simon were quite right in discriminating between these two countries, and Lord Simon would surely have some difficulty now in supporting the false ethics of his earlier attitude.

This chapter illustrates one of the most glaring paradoxes of the international trade in arms: the arms-producing countries which have suffered most from Japanese aggression are just those which have contributed most towards making her a major military Power. During the years leading up to the entry of the United States into this war, the Royal Dutch and Standard Oil groups were mainly responsible for oil supplies to Japan. The Dutch East Indies, now completely subjugated by Japan, was that nation's second largest supplier of both oil and rubber. The largest exporter to Japan of the six most important war materials needed for the support of her armies was America, who poured into the laps of her militarists a never-ending stream of oil, scrap iron, machinery, copper, aircraft and automobiles.

The British Empire concentrated on the supply of non-ferrous metals, rubber, leather, ores and exclusive supplies of asbestos and mica, sending Japan in 1938 more than 91% of her tin, 97·62% of her nickel, 45·97% of her aluminium, 54·29% of her lead, 67·38% of her zinc, 67·65% of her rubber, 60·43% of her leather, 68·77% of her ores, 100% of her asbestos and 100% of her mica. In that year the British Empire and America between them supplied Japan with 76·69% of her war materials and 60·1% of the foreign exchange with which she bought these materials. In point of fact, over 85% of materials essential to war came from the four democratic groups—the U.S.A., the Dutch Empire, the British Empire and the French Empire. The Axis groups, on the other hand, supplied only 3·36% in 1937 and 8·64% in 1938! It is of interest to notice that although the Soviet Union possessed an abundance of some of the war materials required by Japan she sold nothing to her during either 1937 or 1938.

The stream of war supplies went on until almost the last moment. In 1940, America placed a ban on the shipment of high-octane gasoline and aviation lubricating oil, but still the export of oil to Japan increased in that year by $10,000,000. In the same period the export of semi-manufactured iron and steel rose by 100%. In the first three months of 1941 the United States sold Japan more than $4,500,000 worth of copper and $11,706,000 worth of gasoline and oil.

As late as two years after the beginning of the war, the Australian dockers at Port Kembla, New South Wales, struck against the dispatch of loads of pig-iron and steel to Japan by Broken Hill Proprietary—a British-owned company. The strike was ruthlessly broken by the authorities, and the material was shipped as originally intended. It was probably used, with so much of the other material supplied by the democracies, to tear to pieces the bodies of the Aussies, and other troops from the Dominions, Colonies and from America only a few months after the strike.

This Letter Stopped Arms to Japan

In December, 1940, a more successful move was made in this country to stem the flow of this "bloody traffic" to our future enemy. After consultations with one of the present writers, the following letter was written to the Minister of Labour by the Secretary of a Works Committee in the North of England:—

The Right Honourable Ernest Bevin,
Montague House,
Whitehall, S.W.1.

"DEAR SIR,

"I am writing on behalf of the Works Committee at ——. You will probably know that this firm claims to be the 'largest machine cut gear specialists in the world'. It employs approximately 2,000 workpeople.

"Jobs are passing through various stages of manufacture here, the blueprints of which bear the imprint 'Subject to Japanese army inspection'.[1] In view of the association of Japan with the Axis powers, employees on the night shift have refused to handle the job.

"So far the work has been done by the day shift, but considerable discussion and disquiet have occurred. When representatives of the workers interviewed the managers on the matter, Mr. ——, a director of the firm, informed them that the company had a Government licence and that the work must be done in order to maintain export trade.

"The matter has been discussed by the Works Committee, and representatives to the number of twenty have refused to handle the work.

"Messrs. —— are continually making appeals to their employees to increase output in the name of 'patriotism and loyalty'. The employees have responded, but the members of the Works Committee want to say to you emphatically that they are not prepared to co-operate in assisting output to the Japanese army. The British Government has recently reopened the Burma Road so that war material can reach the Chinese armies. What is the use of doing this if British industry is producing war material for the Japanese army? The British Government has recently refused recognition to the Puppet

---

[1] They were, in fact, essential parts of tanks.

Government set up by Japan in China. What is the use of doing this if British industry is to help Japan maintain that Government against the bona fide Chinese Government?

"The American Government has recently extended a large credit to the Chinese Government. What will the Americans think of us if they know we are providing goods for the Japanese army? The Japanese Government is associated by treaty with the Hitler and Mussolini Governments, and it is not unlikely that before the end of the war the Japanese armed forces will be in action against the British forces. Do you think that British workers want to be making articles that would arm the Japanese forces under such conditions?

. "Moreover, what guarantee have we, or have our employers, or have the Government, that work which we do for the Japanese army will not be passed on by the Japanese Government to their friends, the Nazis?

"For our part we are determined not to help Hitler's allies in this way, and we expect you, not only as Minister of Labour, but as member of the War Cabinet, not to allow us to suffer in consequence.

"We ask that you will make an immediate inquiry into this matter and take up with the department concerned the question of the granting of licences for work for the Japanese army.

"We shall expect to hear from you within a few days, as the matter is urgent.

Faithfully yours,

Secretary of the Works Committee."

The Minister of Labour replied that he considered the letter most important and would make immediate inquiries. Meanwhile a Government official visited the factory concerned and insisted that the work be completed. After some time had elapsed, however, the Prime Minister announced that a consignment of war materials for Japan had been stopped and that no further supplies from this country would be allowed to go to Japan.

*   *   *   *   *

D 2

The following news item, taken from *Time* of March 1, 1943, shows that even during war-time the bloody traffic goes on—in this instance in favour of the Allies!

". . . But all Malayan rubber was not lost to the U.S. Last week it was learned that a small trickle has begun to come to U.S. ports once more—via Japan and Russia. Tokyo, saddled with a mountainous surplus, sells it to the Soviet Union; Russia again trades it for U.S. war goods which she needs to fight Japan's allies in Europe. Some day, Malayan rubber from Japan might roll again down Singapore's wide streets under the U.S. flag. Meanwhile, the world has another example of a paradox of international war and commerce— how to trade, at second hand, with the enemy."

Men on either side kill and are killed; the profit-makers draw their dividends from the death and destruction of both sides.

CHAPTER VI

BUSINESS WITH BERLIN

"Will the Germans go to war again? I don't think there is any doubt about it, and the curious thing about it is that I am almost persuaded that some day we shall have to let the Germans arm or we shall have to arm them. With the Russians armed to the teeth, and the tremendous menace in the East, Germany unarmed in the middle is always going to be a plum waiting for the Russians to take. One of the greatest menaces to peace in Europe today is the totally unarmed condition of Germany."

Sir Arthur Balfour, chairman of Capital Steel Works, Sheffield, on October 24, 1933.[1]

"The present situation in Germany is beginning to change from past conditions. It seems pretty clear that Germany is about ready to insist on reasonable armament programmes which will undoubtedly include aircraft. In the meanwhile, Luft Hansa are beginning to expand their programme. It seems reasonable and possible that within the next five years the German Government will provide itself, both for military and commercial purposes, with a considerable amount of new equipment. Naturally, all of this equipment would have to be manufactured in Germany, and I am sure we could never sell direct for such a programme. This may mean that royalties in the next five years might amount to a reasonable sum."

Memo. from president of Pratt and Whitney Aircraft Co. to other officials of the company, February 6, 1933.[2]

NOTE THE dates on which these two statements were made. The distinguished English manufacturer expressed his rather peculiar views nearly a year after Hitler had seized power, and many months after Nazi Germany had openly announced its intention to flout the Treaty of Versailles and to rearm. The American "patriot" scribbled his gay prognosis just about the time when Hermann Goering was drawing up the blueprint for an invincible *luftwaffe*. Both of these gentlemen were only too well aware of the real character of the Nazi revolution. They, and their colleagues in the Armaments International, had watched the Nordic Fascists bludgeon their way to power over the broken body of German democracy. Some, like Thyssen, Krupp, the Czech firm of Skoda and the French company Schneider-Creusot, had from the beginning aided Hitler with financial and diplomatic support. They all knew—these pedlars of death—that, in the hands of the Nazis, no instrument of destruction and torture would become

[1] In a letter to the *Sheffield Daily Telegraph.*
[2] Nye exhibit 591.

rusty from lack of use. And they tumbled over one another—English, French, American, Czech, Dutch—in their eagerness to equip the New Order for its ultimate onslaught on the English, French, American, Czech, Dutch. *It is a serious statement to have to make, that, in an exhaustive, painstaking study of all the relevant evidence over the years 1933–1938, the present authors have been unable to find a single instance of an Allied armament manufacturer refusing to supply Germany on political grounds.*

The simplest explanation is that the armament-capitalist has no use for political or social expediency. His opposite number in, say, the textile industry has to think very seriously about the consequences of an arbitrary depression of his employees' living standards. The armament manufacturer, on the other hand, can fashion and sell the very instruments which will later be used to wipe out his fellow-countrymen, with not a thought for anything but personal gain.

Today the Merchants of Death are respected, honoured members of society. They are allowed to give speeches and write pamphlets on the part which their particular companies are playing in the fight for freedom and democracy. They make stern statements about the fate that awaits the wicked, aggressive Hun, and they caution their compatriots against being "taken in by this rot about an Other Germany or an anti-Nazi Hun". There has *always* been an Other Germany. Even now, there are millions of passive German anti-Nazis looking forward to the day when they can openly strike a blow for liberation. But there was a time, even after Hitler's seizure of power, when anti-Nazis of all political colours *actively* resisted the New Order. Those who were not condemned to the slow death of the concentration camp were butchered outright by Nazi thugs armed with pistols and "Tommy" guns. Where did Himmler's jack-booted assassins get their weapons? *From the "arsenal" of democracy!* Here is an extract from a letter by William N. Taylor, Paris representative of E.I. du Pont de Nemours, to one of the company's officials in America. The date is January 9, 1933:—

"There is a certain amount of contraband among the river shippers, mainly in arms from America. Arms of all kinds coming from America are transhipped in the Scheldt to river barges before the vessels arrive in Antwerp. Then they can be carried through Holland without police inspection or interference. The Hitlerists , . . . are presumed to get arms in this manner. The principal arms coming from America are Thompson sub-machine-guns and revolvers. The number is great. . . . So far I have kept away from these smugglers, but I am going to Hamburg at the first reasonable opportunity and call on them to see what information I can get about the business."[1]

We have already seen how interested the president of Pratt & Whitney Aircraft Co, was in Goering's air programme. His reference to royalties concerned payments made to his company by the Bavarian Motor Works, who were given a licence to manufacture the "Hornet" aero engine for Goering's young men. The original basis was fixed at $200 an engine, but altered, twelve months later, to a lump-sum annual payment of $50,000—regardless of the number of aero-engines manufactured in Germany. But Goering wanted to get his hands on good aero-engines as quickly as possible and, contrary to the expectations voiced in the above letter, was prepared to buy directly from America, or from any other country that was prepared to help him in his work. In 1932, Pratt & Whitney sold only $6,000 worth of their products direct to Germany. For 1933 the figure was $272,000, and in the first eight months of 1934 sales rose to $1,445,000. This last figure covered the export of 176 aero-engines, two large Boeing transports and six two-seater planes of a type easily convertible into light bombers.

During the American inquiry, Senator Nye said it was generally recognized in the trade that enough American equipment was being delivered to Germany at that time to equip 100 planes a

[1] Nye exhibit 507. On January 11, 1933, W. T. Neill of Federal Laboratories wrote to Cowdrey & Co., a firm of New York brokers:—

"Kindly refer to your letter of January 9 in which you ask for more details on our inquiry for 4,000 Craig rifles. . . . We are dealing through a broker who states that his principals are negotiating from Berlin. Just what the ultimate destination of these rifles would be he does not claim to know. We regret, therefore, that we cannot supply this information. . . . A quotation was also desired on 7,000,000 rounds of ammunition for these rifles."

month. That this was no exaggeration is clear from a letter written by one of the Pratt & Whitney officials on October 27, 1933, in which he envisaged the possibility of Germany manufacturing 700 to 800 engines a year on the company's licence alone.[1] At the same time another American company—Sperry Gyroscope—was exporting to Germany enough automatic pilots, gyro-compasses and other instruments to equip at least fifty planes a month.

British airplane companies were just as active; and in the House of Commons on May 14, 1934, Sir John Simon admitted that an order from a German firm for eighty aero-engines had been placed with the Armstrong-Siddeley Co.[2] The French Ambassador had complained about it, but Sir John ("Hands off Japan") Simon went on to explain that "the export of these engines does not conflict with the terms of the relevant international instruments". Later in the year Mr. Stanley Baldwin admitted, in answer to a Parliamentary question, that a further German order had been placed with another British company. Asked whether the Government proposed to take any action in the matter, Mr. Baldwin replied: "The answer is in the negative".

By this time armaments and vital war materials were pouring into Germany in a never-ceasing flood. The National Shipbuilders' Securities organization (the murderers of Jarrow) sold 1,500,000 tons of machinery to the Nazi industrialists at scrap prices and British financiers lent Germany the money with which to buy it. De Havilland Aircraft Company was selling Tiger Moth planes (for naval and military training) to Germany and Japan.[3] Vickers was inserting full-page advertisements of field-guns and tanks in German military journals—advertisements which, according to the Company's chairman, Sir Herbert Lawrence, were inserted "with the complete sanction and

---

[1] Nye exhibit 595.
[2] "Armstrong-Siddeley aircraft engines were sold to Germany in 1934. In consequence, the nascent German air force could start designing its military machines with the results of 16 years of British Government research at its disposal." (Noel Baker, *The Private Manufacture of Armaments*, p. 195.)
[3] Victor Gollancz, *Shall Our Children Live or Die?*, p. 85.

approval of the British Government".[1] I.C.I. was collaborating on the friendliest of terms with the great German chemical combines on which the entire Nazi war effort was dependent.

THE McGOWAN PLAN

The two last-mentioned companies deserve a chapter to themselves, but we must be content with some of the more striking evidence of the assistance which they rendered to Hitler. Some interesting comments on Vickers are made in U.S. Ambassador Dodd's published diary of his tenure of office in Berlin. Here are two extracts:—

I

October 19, 1934. "I visited Sir Eric Phipps and repeated in all confidence a report that Armstrong-Vickers, the great British armament concern, had negotiated a sale of war material here (Berlin) last week, just before the British Government Commission arrived to negotiate with Schacht for payment of $5,000,000 due on current deliveries of British cotton yarn from Manchester. It is impossible, Schacht said to me yesterday, to pay the British debts. Yet last Friday, I reported to Sir Eric, the British arms people were selling for cash enormous quantities of war supplies. And I was frank enough— or indiscreet enough—to add that I understood that representatives of Curtiss Wright from the United States were here this week to negotiate similar sales. The British Ambassador pretended to be surprised. . . ."[2]

[1] John Hargrave, *Professor Skinner, alias Montagu Norman*, p. 220.
[2] John Hargrave's book throws some interesting light on the Nazis' cash payments for British armaments. For example:—

"In May, 1934, a private conference took place between Dr. Schacht and Governor Norman. Then came the 'secret conclave' at Badenweiler in the Black Forest on June 11, when Norman again met Dr. Schacht for an 'unofficial discussion'. They were both on their way to a meeting of the Bank of International Settlements at Basle. Nazi Germany needed a big loan. Early in October, these two met once more at the same Black Forest rendezvous and again the secret negotiations for the support of Hitlerism were discussed and carried a step further. To his English associates, Governor Norman spoke of the political situation in Europe. A new Power had established itself as a great stabilizing force, namely Nazi Germany. The

II

December 10, 1934. "Ebbutt (*Times*) confirmed the report of mid-October that a British woman, connected with Hitler's inner group, was here just before the British negotiations on Lancashire debts to sell war equipment for Armstrong-Vickers. The British Ambassador 'had not known about it', according to previous conversations. I am sure now the British staff members did know."

It is hardly surprising that, between 1931 and 1936, the value of Vickers stock rose by £19,704,000.

The initiative in the rebuilding of the German chemical industry after the last war came from the present Lord McGowan. In 1926, Lord McGowan (then Sir Harry) effected a merger between Brunner-Mond Co., Ltd., and Nobel Industries, Ltd., out of which was born the chemical colossus I.C.I. In a letter dated December 17, 1926, from the London office of E.I. du Pont de Nemours to the du Pont Nitrate Co., it was stated :—

". . . Sir Harry explained that the formation of I.C.I. is only the first step in a comprehensive scheme which he has in mind to rationalize chemical manufacture of the world. The details of such a scheme are not worked out, not even in Sir Harry's own mind, but the broad picture includes working arrangements between three groups—the I.G. in Germany, Imperial Chemical Industries in the British Empire, and du Pont and the Allied Chemical & Dye in America. . . . He hopes to develop some scheme involving financial ties binding the three groups together." [1]

Hitler regime was the only real bulwark against Soviet Russia and the spread of Communism. Hitlerism was no temporary nightmare, but a system of planned economy with a great future before it. Norman advised his co-workers to include Hitler in their plans for financing Europe. There was no opposition. . . . It is quite certain Norman did all he could to assist Hitlerism to gain and maintain political power, operating on the financial plane from his office in Threadneedle Street. Dr. Schacht and Governor Norman were a Dr. Jekyll and Mr. Hyde combination. It worked perfectly for Hitler and orthodox finance."

[1] U.S. Senate Report No. 944, Part 3, p. 221.

The McGowan plan soon began to take shape. I.C.I. and du Pont acquired shares in I.G. Farbenindustrie, and these three trusts together controlled the German explosives company D.A.G. (Dynamit-Actien-Gesellschaft). A gentleman's agreement ensured that each partner in the chemical cartel would disclose to the other its secret inventions relating to explosives. They then proceeded to hammer out a thoroughgoing and comprehensive plan for the division of sales territory and the "rigging" of prices throughout the world. The cartel came to an interesting arrangement for the sale of explosives in South America. A jointly-owned company, Explosives Industries, Ltd., was set up to handle all sales in this territory and quotas were fixed for each of the three partners. *Under this arrangement, the German company was compensated by the British and American companies whenever its sales fell below the allotted quota.* Further, in order to strengthen the German company's position inside its own country, I.C.I. and du Pont paid large sums by way of compensation to certain smaller German companies for withdrawing from and limiting their activities in the export markets.

The restrictions imposed on German chemical concerns by the Versailles Treaty were irksome to the Anglo-American partners. In the first place, I.C.I. and du Pont were obliged to maintain expensive sales organizations in Europe for the exploitation of military business which would normally have been handled by I.G. on the customary profit-sharing basis. Secondly, the mere existence of a ban on the export of military explosives to Germany strengthened "sales resistance" among the neighbouring European States, and constituted the greatest single obstacle in the way of expansion of armament sales. Hitler's advent to power in January, 1933, brought new hope to the distinguished powder pedlars of Britain and America. On February 1, 1933, du Pont signed a contract with a Mr. Peter Brenner (alias Giera), an international agent,[1] under which Brenner was to act as special

[1] During his evidence before the Nye Committee, Mr. Casey, an official of du Pont, admitted to Senator Clark that Giera was generally known as an international spy. Casey answered in the affirmative when Senator Clark suggested that Giera had been an agent for thirteen different Governments, including the German and Japanese.

agent of du Pont "for the Kingdom of Holland and as its exclusive agent for the Republic of Germany, to negotiate the sale of military propellants and military explosives to purchasers located in said territories".[1] It will be recalled that, a month earlier, du Pont's Paris agent had written to America about the bootlegging of war material to Germany through Holland and had announced his intention of calling on the smugglers "to see what information I can get about the business". An individual described by Brenner as "Count Westarp of the German General Staff" was present at the signing of the original contract, which contained no reservation whatsoever respecting the restrictions laid down in the Treaty of Versailles and, by reference, in the treaty of peace between the United States and Germany. Sir Harry McGowan was immediately informed of this contract in a letter from Lammot du Pont which read (in part) as follows:—

"We have made an agreement with Mr. E. D. Giera looking toward the sale of military propellants to the Republic of Germany. . . . For various reasons we desire this matter considered confidential, but particularly so because we feel that any knowledge of such an agreement leaking out might get to some parties whose interest it would be to block Mr. Giera's efforts."[2]

McGowan's reply, dated March 6, 1933, indicated grave doubts as to the feasibility of such an arrangement:—

". . . Although our German friends [I.G. and D.A.G.] have been out of the export military business for many years, they probably have manufactured for local requirements, and I think we may assume that they have not been idle in their research. It is definitely established that they have not been so in military detonators. I feel sure that when freedom to manufacture is granted for home use and possibly for export, they will expect to take a prominent position in the business, and one which will be in keeping with our arrangement with them on blasting explosives, and we have in fact kept in mind

[1] Nye exhibits 519, 520.
[2] Nye Hearings, Part 5, p. 1237.

this possibility. If the agent you have appointed, therefore, is at all active, I think that any future negotiations would tend to become more difficult, and the Germans would probably consider that, as we reserve to ourselves orders from our respective Governments, they would be entitled to do likewise." [1]

The letter was a clear hint to du Pont that any outside competition with their German partners might jeopardize future cartel relations. The hint was taken, and Brenner was given an assignment in Japan plus $25,000 as compensation. The fact of the matter was that the relationship at that time between I.C.I. and I.G. was too harmonious and mutually advantageous to admit of any unnecessary friction. Two years earlier I.C.I. had joined with I.G., Royal Dutch Shell and the Standard Oil group to form International Hydrogenation Patents Co., a "world brains trust" to develop the production of synthetic petrol from coal. At the Royal Commission inquiry of 1936, a chemical scientist testified to the military value of the hydrogenation process by citing the huge subsidy paid by the Government to I.C.I., by exempting such petrol from duty; but the interchange of information with the German I.G. continued right up to the outbreak of the present war.

* * * * *

So far, we have only scratched the surface of the aid which Hitler received from the nationals of those countries on which he was preparing to unleash all the horrors of modern war. The full extent of this aid can never be recorded, for the relationship between the known and the unknown facts of the bloody traffic is very much the same as that between the visible and invisible sections of an iceberg. That shrewd, far-seeing business-men should go out of their way to put a pistol in the hands of the megalomaniac Hitler need occasion no surprise; for it was *because* of their shrewdness rather than in spite of it that they chose to follow such a policy. Directors of armament companies are, first and foremost, interested in profits. The greater the volume of sales, the greater must be the volume of profits. It is logical, therefore, that they should look with a benevolent eye on Hitler's

[1] Nye Hearings, Part 5, pp. 1243–1244.

rearmament activities, for here was at once a source of increased export business and world-wide political apprehension. In effect, every plane sent to Germany created a potential demand for another plane by their own Government, and from 1933 onwards, the armament companies set out to exploit this situation to the full. In this connection, the cynicism shown by the chairman of Handley Page at the company's annual general meeting of 1934 is worthy of note:—

> "The directors note with satisfaction that, on the breaking down of the Disarmament Conference, the Government had decided on increasing the Air Force to bring it more into line with other nations.
>
> ". . . During the year under review *we have delivered aircraft to four foreign Governments.*
>
> ". . . The future of the Empire demands an Air Force equal to that of any other. *The disparity with the strength of other Powers is disturbing.*" (Our italics.)[1]

We will let the curtain down on this infamous chapter in the history of the bloody traffic with a quotation from the *News Chronicle:*—

> "Huge German orders for rubber and copper were executed in London yesterday, regardless of cost. The buying of nearly 3,000 tons of copper sent the price rocketing up 18s. 9d. to £44 18s. 9d. a ton. Already Germany has bought over 10,000 tons this month in London alone."

The date? August 19, 1939.

[1] Oliver Brown, *Arms and the Men*, p. 16.

CHAPTER VII

PATRIOTISM, LTD.

It is a moot point whether the armament manufacturer is more to be pitied than despised. He does not want the horrors of war any more than you or we want them. He only wants the profits of war; and if he could get the profits without the horrors he would be as happy as a dog with two tails. Unfortunately for his peace of mind, war profits and war horrors must always go hand in hand. He is thus faced with a perpetual conflict between his own interests and those of society at large—a conflict which can be resolved to his own satisfaction only (*a*) by withdrawing from the armaments industry, or (*b*) by attempting to rationalize his position. We have yet to hear of an armament manufacturer who has failed to seek self-justification on grounds ranging from eugenics to patriotism.

In this chapter we shall attempt to expose the shallowness and superficiality of the hoary argument that an arms merchant is automatically a "patriot" and the "main pillar of his country's national defence structure". We shall adduce evidence to show that, as a general rule, the armament-capitalist is impelled by the very nature of his calling to tread the path of private gain rather than that of patriotic self-sacrifice. During this war a minority, whose existence cannot be denied, has substantially proved its willingness to put the national interest first; but insofar as they make this choice *they are bad capitalists and unrepresentative of their class.*

Before examining the war-time activities of some of these self-styled patriots, let us take a brief glance at their record during the rearmament period leading up to the outbreak of hostilities. Between 1932 and 1938, Britain spent £1,298,000,000 on armaments. What was the result? According to "Scrutator", writing in the *Sunday Times* on October 19, 1941:—

"The B.E.F. was short of ammunition, of anti-tank guns, of armour-piercing shells and of many kinds of anti-aircraft material. Our only armoured division arrived too late to participate, and of the B.E.F.'s tanks no more than 23 were of a type that could stand up in a duel against the German panzers."

And in the House of Commons on July 25, 1939, Mr. J. J. Davidson (M.P. for Maryhill) stated :—

"The Government Chief Whip, when asked about the anti-aircraft units, told us that the position in Scotland *was very satisfactory,* and when Hon. Members asked for information he told us that there were *two anti-aircraft units in the whole country.* . . . I have been informed that after many months Glasgow has now one balloon, and it has been lent to Glasgow by London."

Later in the discussion, Commander Fletcher asked : "When do we get our balloons back for London?" To which Captain Balfour replied : "Let me at once answer the Hon. and Gallant Gentleman that *not one effective balloon* has been taken from London". In other words, all that Scotland could show for this vast expenditure on national defence was two anti-aircraft units and a barrage of one balloon, presumably defective!
One explanation for this appalling scandal was given in *John Bull* on May 7, 1938 :—

"M.P.s for industrial districts, who are well aware of what is going on, openly declare that there is a tremendous amount of fraud and swindling. They are prepared to name firms which are being allowed to amass wealth quickly. Because the Government is either impotent or quiescent, their accusations are merely ignored."

In this country, substantiated evidence of armament scandals *after* September, 1939, is exceedingly difficult to obtain. In part, this is undoubtedly due to the alacrity with which the various Government departments handle these cases before news can filter out and affect public morale. But the greatest single factor militating against a proper exposure of war produciton scandals lies in the extraordinary extent to which Big Business has taken over all the key positions in the various departments concerned with supply and the allocation of contracts.[1] In most of their day-to-day business, the directors of armament companies are dealing directly with men who share their outlook on all the essential aspects of production-for-profit. *Indeed, in many instances, they are dealing with former colleagues who are still drawing dividends from the firms concerned and who hope, after the war, to return to prosperous and well-established enterprises.* It would not be surprising, in the circumstances, if these part-time Government officials were prepared to display a little more tolerance in the matter of war contract "irregularities" than would be expected from established Civil Servants. Even so, anyone who is prepared to examine Press files and Parliamentary reports covering the war-time years will find abundant evidence of swindling and profiteering by these so-called "patriots" and "public-spirited" industrialists.

Sometimes it is the workers who blow the gaff. For example: in October, 1943, shop stewards at a Vickers Armstrong aircraft factory in the Home Counties announced that they were dissatisfied with what they regarded as the poor output from this factory. They alleged that when Sir Stafford Cripps visited the works earlier in the month, the management deliberately tried to deceive the Minister by "window-dressing of the most flagrant kind in the erecting shop". *For many weeks*, it was alleged, *production in that department had been almost at a standstill, with many workers only half employed or on waiting cards.*

The bulk of the evidence is buried in the poorly publicized reports of the Select Committee on National Expenditure, the Controller and Auditor-General on National Expenditure, the Committee of Public Accounts, etc. For example: within a few days of the Vickers shop stewards' statement the last-mentioned committee gave details of some of the exorbitant profit margins made on the building of warships for the British Navy. The committee inquired into the profit rates yielded by contracts for the hull and machinery of warships ordered from 1936 to 1939.

---

[1] See Appendix.

These contracts—some of which, we must assume, were not finally adjusted until after the outbreak of war—covered 32 warships—a battleship, an aircraft carrier, cruisers, destroyers, submarines and smaller craft, *representing about a quarter of the ships ordered during the period*. The total cost at contract prices, including profit, was about £900 millions.

The results disclosed were that in four cases the profit on cost was less than 10%. [7% is generally considered to be a fair profit on warship construction.] *In five cases profits were between 10% and 20%; in nine between 20% and 30%; in seven between 30% and 40%; in two between 40% and 50%; in one between 50% and 60%; in one between 60% and 70%; in two between 70% and 80%, and in one over 80%*. The report added that "in recent years the Public Accounts Committee have on several occasions had their attention drawn to a number of cases in which prices certified by [the Government's] technical departments to be *fair and reasonable* have been shown by cost investigations to be *excessive*".

The Civil Appropriation Accounts for 1942–43 give an analysis of the profits made by 3,300 firms working on war contracts for the various Government Departments. Of these 3,300 firms, 1,300 are large companies with capital of £50,000 and over. The analysis shows that 25% of these firms made profits on costs up to 15%, 35% made profits of between 15% and 30%, *and 38% made profits of over 30%*. The Auditor-General adds that arrangements have been made with 149 firms to refund £4,700,000 of the excessive profits acquired from these contracts. When a miner demands a few shillings a week more for toiling in the bowels of the earth, he is accused by the Government, the Press and the employers of "holding the community up to ransom". Today he can be imprisoned for using, or threatening to use the only weapon he has—the strike. There is no threat of imprisonment to deter the chair-borne divisions of Big Business from swindling the community to the extent of millions of pounds. At the worst, they are asked to "refund" their ill-gotten gains; at the best, their financial manipulations remain forever undetected.

It should be noted that the officials of His Majesty's technical departments are recruited often from the staffs of private firms, who usually show a most co-operative spirit in releasing them from their employ.

This letter, written, before the war, by the chief of Vickers Armstrong (Sir Charles Craven) to our old friend the president of Electric Boat Co., is not without interest:—

"With regard to paragraph 4 of your letter, I wish you the best of luck and hope you may be able to knock out some of your Government dockyards. They seem to be even more of a nuisance with you than they are here. I wonder whether you have heard that our old friend Percy Addison is now the Director of Dockyards. I helped him all I could to get the job, and I think he will be an ideal fellow for it. It means his retirement, but it also means his having a permanent job for about ten years *if he behaves himself,* and as he has no private means worth talking about, *you will appreciate what this means.* I have suggested to him that you and I, and he and John (who is anxious to meet you) should have a party and thoroughly wet the appointment next time you are over here." [Our italics.]

In another letter to his American colleague, Sir Charles Craven wrote:—

". : . We have just received an inquiry for one, two or three boats from the Admiralty. Armstrong Whitworth's [then in the process of being absorbed by Vickers] have also received a similar inquiry. My present feeling is that we should quote for one, two or three from Armstrongs, who have agreed to put in whatever price I tell them, and that we should also quote for one, two or three from Barrow [Vickers' shipyard]. I would keep the Armstrong price very slightly above ours, the idea being that whatever boats were ordered from either party would be built at Barrow. . . . I also think that perhaps it would be worth while putting forward a tender for six boats, the total number to be built. I have had a word with the director of contracts at the Admiralty, who is a friend of mine, and who would like this. He, I know, tried to get us the order for all five submarines last year."

Sir Charles Craven was chosen by the Prime Minister in June, 1941, to be Controller-General at the Ministry of Aircraft Production (a sphere of war industry in which Vickers holds a very high stake). Announcing his appointment on June 13, the *Daily Express* told its readers that *one of Sir Charles' duties was to check profiteering.* After twelve months' experience at the Ministry, Craven resigned the post on medical grounds. He made a rapid recovery, however, and returned to his duties as chairman and managing director of Vickers and English Steel Corporation.

Nothing Too Good for Our Boys

Now let us see how American big business-men have been playing their part in the war to preserve "America's way of living". In the August 23, 1943, issue of the American magazine *Newsweek* there appeared a full-page advertisement which must have sent a glow of pride coursing through the veins of every patriotic American. The top part of the advertisement contained a drawing of the head and shoulders of a young American pilot, looking straight out at the reader with fearless eyes and a grim, determined mouth. In the background was a fighter plane, resting on the ground, its tail badly "shot-up". The young pilot speaks, with the laconic sentimentality of a highly-paid American copy-writer:—

"I want to say a few words to the people back home. They came out of the sun—there were six of them. When they turned back there were only three. . . . As for me, I shouldn't be here to tell it, I guess, but I am. That's why I want to say a few words to the people back home. I want to thank the people who built that plane of mine. Up there, our chances depend upon the sturdiness and workmanship in every part that goes into the planes we fly. It was the plane and the people who built it that gave me another chance."

Then the advertisers—the Curtis Wright Corporation—add their little piece:—

"To that brave American flyer, we at Curtiss Wright have this to say: '. . . No failure on our part shall deprive you of another chance. The finest in skill and workmanship that we know how to give you is our job in this war—building planes in which every part—every single rivet—will help to bring you through.'"

So much for the fiction. Now for the reality. . . .

A month previous to the appearance of this advertisement a Congressional Committee submitted to the War Frauds Division of the Department of Justice charges that the Wright Aeronautical Corporation (a wholly-owned subsidiary of Curtiss Wright) was "producing and causing the Government to accept defective, sub-standard and unsatisfactory aeroplane motor materials". Forgery of inspection reports and skipping of inspections were also alleged. The report stated that a "substantial number" of planes using engines made in the company's Lockland factory had had crashes in which engine failures were involved, that more than 25% of the engines built at the plant failed in one or more major parts during three-hour test runs, and that spare parts were shipped without proper inspection. The day following the publication of the Congressional Committee's report, Mr. Robert Patterson, U.S. Under-Secretary of War, said that the Army's own investigation found "a falling off in inspection procedures" at the Curtiss Wright factory and "confirmed the greater part of the information furnished by the Truman Committee".

It is interesting that, although Curtiss Wright held, at that time, the second largest war contracts in America, Press criticism was largely confined to the small number of American Left-wing newspapers and periodicals. Under a banner headline "CURTISS WRIGHT CAUGHT REDHANDED", the *Militant* of New York wrote:—

"The Truman report shows that profits, and not the patriotic sentiments expressed in advertisements, are the first concern of

Curtiss Wright. Its officials want to win the war . . . but far more important to them is the coining of more and more profits at a faster and faster rate, regardless of the consequences to the welfare of the workers in the plants and the servicemen in battle. The speed with which Government officials and powerful newspapers have rushed to the defence of Curtiss Wright is an admission that its outlook is shared by Big Business as a whole. The Truman report, therefore, constitutes a damning indictment not only of Curtiss Wright and the other companies engaged in similar criminal practices but of the entire capitalist class."

And the New York daily, *PM*, wrote:—

". . . ask yourself if this country shouldn't have a law enabling it to shoot as traitors all those who are responsible for selling out the war effort for gain."

How *are* these Big Business swindlers treated by their Big Business Government? The usual "penalty" is the imposition of a fine whose effect has been compared by Senator Bone to "a slap on the wrist". An example of this was provided only two days after the exposure of the Curtiss Wright case, when the Sandusky Foundry and Machinery Company of Ohio was let off with a fine of $80,000 *after pleading guilty to faking its tests and selling the Government sub-standard propellor sleeves for use in Navy vessels.* But an even more farcical penalty was imposed on another powerful company for a war fraud which was described as "the most obnoxious ever presented to a court of the United States".

During the critical battles fought by the Red Army in 1942, it was found that vital communications were constantly being endangered by faulty wires. An investigation was made, and towards the end of the year the Soviet authorities complained to America *that 50% of the wire manufactured by the Anaconda Wire and Cable Co. and exported under Lend-Lease was defective.* At the company's trial in June, 1943, thirty-nine witnesses described how inspection tags had been changed from specially tested prepared cable to cable which had not been tested. Twenty witnesses told of a system of hidden "circuit boxes" which fooled Government inspectors, and one witness testified that an official of the company, Mr. Frank E. Hart, told him: "Don't get caught. If you do, it's your neck—not mine or the company's". As it turned out, Mr. Hart was an unreliable prophet, for he was sent to prison with the general manager. But the company, which was found guilty of having fraudulently sold the Government $5,000,000 worth of faulty wire, received a fine of—$10,000.

One of the biggest war-time scandals on the U.S. production front concerns the steel-faking activities of the Carnegie Illinois Steel Corporation. Suspicions that all was not as it should be in this company's testing departments were aroused when the 16,500-ton tanker *Schenectady* broke in two and sank only a few hours after it had been delivered to the Maritime Commission on January 17, 1943. A report on the incident by the American Bureau of Shipping stated that the plates on the *Schenectady* were "brittle" and "more like cast iron than steel". At a hearing before the Truman Senate Investigating Committee in Washington on March 23 it was estimated that fake tests ordered by the company's officials covered at least 28,000 to 30,000 tons of substandard plate. The testimony of one witness was that, at a single Carnegie Illinois plant, records were faked on about 5% of its 60,000-ton monthly capacity, resulting in the acceptance by the Government each month of about 3,000 tons of steel plate which would normally have been rejected. In a written statement put before the committee, George E. Dye, supervisor of inspection at the company's Irvin works, wrote:—

"Since July, 1942, I have been aware that the mill was shipping badly laminated and piped plates to the U.S. Navy and U.S. maritime shipping yards and that defective steel was being supplied on U.S. Treasury Lend-Lease orders."

Dye, repeatedly complained to his superiors that bad plates were being shipped, and finally, in November, 1942, he received instructions from William F. McGarrity, chief metallurgist of the company's Edgar Thompson works, to prevent shipment of substandard plates.

"Two days later", Dye continued, "John McConnell (sheet mill metallurgist inspector) told me that McGarrity 'got his ears beat back' when he brought the subject up in an operating meeting, and I was instructed to go easy on rejections."

Carnegie Illinois is an old hand at the profitable game of faking steel tests. In 1894, after the Carnegie Steel company had admitted that it deliberately sold defective armour plate to the United States Navy, the House of Representatives Naval Affairs Committee reported that:—

"The company, or its servants, have perpetrated manifold frauds, the natural tendency of which was to palm off on the Government an inferior armour, whose inferiority might perchance appear only in the shock of battle, and with incalculable damage to the country. No fine or mere money compensation is an adequate atonement for such wrongs. The commission of such frauds is a moral crime of the gravest character.

"If the criminality of a wrongful act is to be measured by the deliberation with which it is committed, the magnitude of the evils likely to result from its perpetration, and the want of provocation with which it is done, the frauds which your committee have found are worthy to be crimes."

Less widely known, but not less sordid than the Carnegie case is the extraordinary story of Admiral Land and the Higgins shipbuilding contract. Admiral Emory S. Land is the man who, in April, 1943, was reappointed by the U.S. Senate for a six-year term as chairman of the U.S. Maritime Commission. He is known as the "old-line" shipbuilders' fairy godfather and American Labour's bitterest enemy: it was he who declared on October 19, 1942, that "every labour organizer should be shot at sunrise".

When America came into the war, it was found that her grandiose shipbuilding plans were not only far from completion, but proved to be entirely inadequate to meet the tremendous demand for vessels. It was in these circumstances that the Maritime Commission entered into a contract with the Higgins Corporation for the construction of a shipyard which, at the peak of operation, would turn out Liberty ships at the then unheard-of rate of two a day. This was to be accomplished by a new assembly-line method worked out by Andrew Higgins, president of the company. The waste, in terms of dollars and labour power, incurred by the ultimate cancellation of this contract was brought to light in a 2,000-page report prepared by a committee of the American Federation of Labour and submitted to President Roosevelt in November, 1942. After stating that the Maritime Commission bought, for $178,000, a 1,200-acre site near New Orleans, commenced to build an 11¼-mile service·canal and ordered 89,366 piles, of which 22,291 were driven in at an additional cost of approximately $25 per pile, the report goes on:—

"Of the estimated 27 miles of railroad track needed within the site, about 3 miles were completed. Materials for the construction of the additional 24 miles were on hand or had been ordered. . . . A steam locomotive and a large number of flat cars had been delivered for use on the plant's railroad. Hundreds of huge trucks, about 100 huge busses, dozens of crates, and a large number of heavy and light tools and equipment had been delivered to the Higgins Corporation and were on the site. Huge quantities of both heavy and light equipment and many thousands of feet of electric wire and cable had also been delivered. Twenty thousand tons of structural steel were ordered for the plant . . . nearly all of which had to be specially fabricated. . . . The Louisville and Nashville Railroad doubled about 12 miles of its track from the city of New Orleans to the site. . . . Telephone, power and other utilities acted rapidly . . . more than $50,000 was spent by the New Orleans Public Service Corporation on power facilities. . . . New Orleans merchants stocked up with merchandise. . . . Tragic losses were sustained by many families who sold their homes in other parts of the country to come to New Orleans."

Within a short time the Maritime Commission had expended in orders and commitments "a total of $30,000,000". An idea of the size of the project can be gained from the fact that "seven hydraulic dredges and four clamshell dredges were assembled— making one of the largest concentrations of such equipment in history, greater than the amount of that type of equipment used in the construction of the Panama Canal".

According to the A.F. of L. report, the Higgins system of construction would reduce the man-hours required in the construction of a Liberty ship from the existing average of 500,000 to 230,000 or less. "On the basis of an average labour cost of $1 per hour in shipbuilding plants, the Government would have saved in labour costs alone on these ships at least a quarter of a million dollars on each vessel launched." Thus, on the initial order of 200 ships the Government would have saved more than enough to have paid for the construction of the shipyard. In comparison with other shipyards, the Higgins plant could "have saved our nation $180,000,000 annually"; and "the Higgins yard and the Kaiser yard together could have produced the entire 15,000,000 tons of shipping ordered by President Roosevelt for the year 1943. . . . The evidence before this committee established conclusively that no shipyard in the country could have competed in cost, speed or labour savings with the Higgins yard."

But it was this very efficiency that alarmed the "old line" shipbuilders, who apparently considered the threat of the Higgins shipyard to be far more critical than the threat of the Axis U-boats. Fortunately, they had a good man "on the inside"—Mr. Joseph W. Powell, of the Bureau of Ships—who was a life-long friend of Admiral Land and a former vice-president of the infamous Bethlehem Shipbuilding Corporation. Powell declared that "no new shipyard would be opened up or financed by the United States Government and that no yards would be financed or constructed except those which would be under the control and management of existing shipbuilding companies". He got to work on his friend the Admiral, who thereupon cancelled the Higgins contract (giving as his reason the "shortage of steel") and distributed the order for 200 Liberty ships among the "old line" builders.

The Admiral's tactics are worthy of note. First, the public relations department of the Maritime Commission was instructed to "soft pedal on Higgins, soft pedal on Kaiser, and build up Bethlehem Steel". He then appointed a certain Mr. J. L. Baker to have full power of approval and rejection over all Higgins activities and expenditures. Several weeks after the project was begun, Higgins followed Baker's recommendation that Brown & Root of Texas take charge of construction. "The performance of Brown & Root on other Government projects had been satisfactory", reported the A.F. of L. committee. Their performance now became so unsatisfactory, and so many delays and troubles ensued, that Higgins finally cancelled the deal. Prior to "the apparently obstructive tactics of Brown & Root", the construction of the facilities had been "proceeding speedily and satisfactorily". Admiral Land then began artificially to create a shortage of steel plates and informed Donald M. Nelson, of the War Production Board, that "if the Higgins contract were cancelled 58,000 tons of steel could be saved". Land exaggerated, since the total required by Higgins was only 29,000 tons, but Nelson approved Land's recommendation and the contract was cancelled.

Later, Donald Nelson appeared before the A.F. of L. committee and succeeded in convincing its members that he was not simply passing the buck in accusing Admiral Land of full responsibility for the cancellation.

"Mr. Nelson stated positively that he would not have given his approval to cancellation . . . if all the facts as he knew them when he appeared before this committee . . . had been known to him at the time of Admiral Land's request for approval. Mr. Nelson was, without doubt, misled into giving his approval. . . . Factual misrepresentations and concealment of material facts were resorted to by Admiral Land in his successful attempt to get Donald M. Nelson to approve the cancellation."

E

THE DIVIDENDS OF DEATH

This chapter would be incomplete if we were to close it without referring to some of the outstanding cases of pure monetary profiteering by American firms which did at least "deliver the goods". The evidence that follows should be read in the light of the U.S. capitalist class's unanimous and ferocious opposition to American Labour's struggle for better wages and conditions. Most of the worst exposures were, in fact, made at the time when American Big Business was accusing the Pennsylvanian miners of "holding up the community to ransom".

According to a committee of the United States Congress, "untold millions of dollars" were being made by war contract profiteers long before America actually came into the war. In a report published at the beginning of 1942, this committee stated that it had evidence that brokers had obtained commissions ranging up to 74% on sub-contracts. An example was given where one New York commission broker, Leon K. Shanack, made a £31,186 profit on £65,916 worth of orders. Seven months after Pearl Harbour, the House of Representatives Naval Affairs Committee revealed that in some cases *profits on individual naval contracts with the Government reached 1,768%.* The committee recommended Congressional action to curb this minority from "enriching themselves at the public expense".

The urgency of the need for legislative action was underlined only a month later when Mr. F. Biddle, U.S. Attorney-General, announced the indictment of six companies for conspiracy to defraud the United States Government by violating the conditions for the sale of insulated cable to the Navy. It was stated that the defendants had made profits of 17–35% on the sales (a "reasonable" average in the United States is 8%), and that one defendant had already returned more than £60,000 to the Navy Departments on contracts involving £500,000. Proportionate returns were expected on other contracts said to involve more than £12,000,000. *During the whole of 1943, the Naval Affairs Committee's study of war contracts resulted in "direct savings of $700,000,000"—all of which would otherwise have gone into the coffers of the armament* *manufacturers.* In making this statement, on January 18, 1943, the committee revealed that 121 war brokers had received $15,000,000 since 1939 in soliciting Government agencies for war business.

The committee's authority to investigate war costs was renewed by Congress, and 1943 saw the uncovering of more scandals of a similarly revolting nature. We have room for one sample from the 1943 crop. The details emerged in evidence taken before the committee in March of that year. It was revealed that a company engaged in the manufacture of airplane starters had reported an average profit of 10%, but that, on investigation, the average turned out to be 100%, or ten times as much! The secretary to the president of the company alone received nearly £10,000 a year, and a former civil servant admitted that after he had been employed by the firm for forty-five days he had received nearly £3,000 in bonuses beside his regular salary of £8,000 a year.

In justice to the millions of ordinary American citizens who hate their profiteering compatriots as much as we hate our own, we reprint the following news item from the New York *Herald Tribune* of January 17, 1942:—

"Judge Charles S. Colden suspended sentence yesterday on Harry Goldberg . . . who had pleaded guilty of forgery in the third degree in Queens County Court, in appropriating $3,250 he obtained on a check he signed as the representative of a furniture company.

" 'Today we are suffering from the shock of the terrible things that we have discovered in the report of the Senate investigating committee', said Judge Colden. 'Men who were supposed to have been men of great character and moral integrity and patriotism have been guilty of things displayed by that report. We find men that are gorging themselves with the wealth that is being contributed by patriotic Americans, so that they can enrich themselves like swine in the feeding trough. We read such things as one man saying that the profits of his company were so great that they needed a steam shovel to handle them.

" 'Until we have a firing squad to take care of people of that kind, we ought not to deal harshly with some foolish individual who has a good record and has been a pretty decent sort of a man and who has made a slip. So today I am going to suspend sentence upon you, Henry Goldberg, upon the understanding that henceforth you will never do anything which will cause you to be brought into court.' "

PARTNERSHIP WITH THE NAZIS

We cannot attempt, in this present book, to make a comprehensive survey of the ramifications and pernicious activities of the international capitalist cartels. Information that has already been brought to light—and there is far more yet to be revealed—proves beyond any shadow of doubt that the Nazi war machine could not possibly have been assembled and put into operation had the German industrialists not been able to count, from 1933 onwards, on the whole-hearted support of their cartel partners in Britain and America. At the time of going to press, the British Government has given no indication that it intends to depart from its traditional policy of supporting the cartel arrangement made between British monopolists and their foreign partners—arrangements which in nearly every instance operate against the real interests of the common man throughout the world. The American Government has at least made a show of concerning itself with the activities of its own monopolists, and, while most of its prosecutions have been suspended until after the war, the public has already been given a preview of the world-wide conspiracy which this war so rudely interrupted, but out of which the war itself was born. Here are some characteristic examples of exposures made in America up to this time:—

I

National Lead Co., linked financially with du Pont, has been indicted on a charge of supplying I. G. Farbenindustrie's South American customers and putting aside a share of the profits to be transferred to I.G. after the war.

II

Standard Oil Co. (the American partner in the German-British-American hydrogenation cartel) has been fined for its refusal—months after America's entry into the war—to release its secret process for the manufacture of butyl rubber, although this process had already been handed over to the Nazis and Italians. Just before Pearl Harbour, a Senate Committee announced that Standard Oil tankers were delivering oil to Teneriffe island for German and Italian use.

III

Dow Chemical has been charged with the deliberate restriction of magnesium production because of its arrangements with the German chemical trusts.

IV

Remington Arms Co., a subsidiary of du Pont, refused to sell tetracene to the British Purchasing Commission in America because of its arrangements with I.G. Farbenindustrie.

It will be noted that the German chemical colossus, I.G., is concerned in all these arrangements for strengthening the hands of German militarists at the expense of the Allies. It might be expected from this that the Governments of America and Britain will refuse to countenance any resumption of cartel relations with I.G. after the war—no matter how innocuous these may at first appear. But they will first have to deal with the managements of combines such as the Standard Oil Co., which, in June, 1943, *defeated a resolution by minority shareholders which sought to prevent the post-war resumption of the company's cartel relations with I.G. Farbenindustrie.*

APPENDIX

On May 13, 1942, the Minister of Supply announced, in the House of Commons, the names of the twenty-five men appointed to control raw materials. *Every one of them represents leading capitalist concerns vitally interested in the allocation of war orders and the supply of rationed materials.* Some of the more interesting appointments are given in the following table:—

Abrasives	Mr. C. J. Brockbank	Brockbank & Powell, Ltd.
Chrome Ore, Magnesite, Wolfram, etc.	Mr. W. T. V. Harmer	United Steel Cos., Ltd.
Diamond Die and Tool	Mr. R. L. Prain	Anglo Metal Co. (Managing Director).
Industrial Ammonia	Mr. F. C. O. Speyer	I.C.I. (Fertilizer & Synthetic Products), Ltd. (Director).
Iron and Steel	Sir Charles Wright	Guest, Keen, Baldwins Iron & Steel Co., Ltd. (Chairman).
Molasses and Industrial Alcohol	Mr. T. F. A. Board	Distillers Co., Ltd.
Non-Ferrous Metals	Mr. W. Mure Mr. A. M. Baer	British Metal Corp. (Both Managing Directors).
Non-Ferrous Mineral Development	Sir William Larke —	Iron & Steel Federation. (Director).
Rubber	Mr. F. D. Ascoli	Dunlop Rubber Plantations, Ltd. (Managing Director).
Sulphuric Acid	Mr. N. G. Thomas	National Sulphuric Acid Association, Ltd.

In answer to a Parliamentary question in July, 1943, the Minister of Supply stated that there were sixty-one former officials of I.C.I. employed in key positions in his department.

CHAPTER VIII

AN END TO DIVIDENDS

In the course of his testimony before the Royal Commission on the Private Manufacture of and Trading in Arms, Mr. William Arnold-Forster, then adviser to the National Peace Council, voiced a truism when he said that "the competitive arms trade is conducted in conditions which offer every inducement and opportunity for secrecy, and usually it is only some accident . . . which flashes an occasional light into the darkness". In the preceding chapters we have grouped together some of the major and minor "flashes" of the past thirty years, believing that their concentrated light will help to dispel any lingering shadows of doubt as to the evils inherent in the practice of private trading in armaments.

Illumination is not, however, the sole objective of this book. It is a sound principle—almost, in fact, a rule of social morality—not to attack an established order or institution unless a more desirable, and thoroughly practical, alternative exists. This, then, is our other objective: to examine the main arguments for and against the present system and to put forward what, in the present writers' considered judgement, are minimum safeguards against any future recrudescence of the bloody traffickers' activities.

At the risk of infuriating the champions of "private enterprise", we will start with the contention that an unanswerable case can be made for the complete expropriation by the State of the entire arms-producing capacity and facilities at present under private control. The immediate benefits of such a move would be the elimination of the profit-motive and the transfer of the onus for foreign transactions to a National Arms Board directly answerable to Parliament and the people.

It is necessary, of course, to draw a clear distinction between nationalization adopted *independently* as a voluntary measure by some or all of the arms-producing States and nationalization *by world agreement*. In the first instance, such nations would be perfectly free, at any time, to revert to private manufacture without consulting other nations; and as long as other important arms-producing countries eschewed nationalization, all the evils of the bloody traffic would remain, although on a somewhat lessened scale. To accept this fact, however, is not to accept the thoroughly discredited argument that isolated measures for the abolition of private manufacture are valueless and against the national interest.[1] *We believe that, in the absence of world agreement, abolition should certainly be effected by Great Britain acting alone.* Anything that represents a step in the right direction is praiseworthy in itself and of incalculable value as a moral lead to other and less forward-looking producing States. And we shall see, shortly, how utterly false and misleading are the arguments that independent abolition of private manufacture need weaken this country's economic and national defence structures.

But obviously, nationalization by world agreement is infinitely preferable to independent nationalization. At one blow, private profit would be taken out of war *everywhere*; and such an agreement, embodying, as it must, mutually agreed limitations on production, would lay the foundations for an ultimate world disarmament programme which, unlike the ill-fated programmes of the past, could not be undermined by the Merchants of Death and their paid hirelings and scribes.

Turning from the theory of nationalization to its practice, let us first consider the nature of the so-called "technical difficulties" which, it has been argued, would make such an operation impossible of achievement. How, in the first place, could the outright abolition of the private manufacture of arms in this country (and by foreign subsidiary companies controlled by British subjects) be effected within the framework of existing legislative machinery? A summary of the necessary measures was laid before the Royal Commission on October 30, 1935, by P. J. Noel Baker.[2]

1. It would be announced by His Majesty's Government that, after a certain date, with probably one or two years' notice :—

[1] This argument was voiced by several leading armament manufacturers called to give evidence before the Nye Committee and the Royal Commission.
[2] Minutes of Evidence, Part 10, p. 297.

(a) no more arms or munitions would be purchased for the British Armed Forces from private firms;

(b) no further licences would be issued to private firms for the export of arms or munitions to foreign countries or to British Dominions overseas.

2. Arms and munitions would be defined in these announcements to mean the articles already listed in the Order in Council of 1931, which now governs the export of war material.

3. Regulations would be prepared and issued laying down the component parts of arms and munitions which private firms would not be allowed to manufacture for the Home Government or for export.

4. Regulations would be issued laying down what specialized machinery for armament production private manufacturers would be forbidden to possess.

5. To prevent the transference of private capital and private experts to foreign countries where private manufacture might not have been abolished, the Government should also forbid any British subject:

(a) to invest capital in armament production in foreign countries or in British Dominions overseas;

(b) to take service in private firms engaged in armament production in foreign countries or in British Dominions overseas;

(c) to engage in any form of private trade or commerce in arms or munitions of war, whether at home or abroad;

(d) to enter the employment of national arsenals in foreign countries or British Dominions overseas without the previous consent of His Majesty's Government in the United Kingdom.

6. The above decisions would be made legally effective by Order in Council or by Parliamentary legislation as the Law Officers of the Crown might find to be necessary. Offences against these Orders in Council or Statutes would be made punishable by heavy penalties, including, if necessary, the loss of British nationality.

E 2

Two important loopholes in Noel Baker's proposals must be closed before we can accept them as constituting an adequate legislative framework. The Order in Council mentioned in the second measure permits the unlicensed export of aero engines for civilian aircraft and of chemical substances used in the production of poison gas. The use to which Nazi Germany put the first type of product and Japan the second must guide the Government's Law Officers in the drafting of a new and really comprehensive Order. The second loophole exists in Part (a) of the fifth measure. To be fully effective, this measure must require the sale of any shares *already held* in foreign armament concerns and must make it illegal for any British subject to acquire such shares in any circumstances (a ban on the direct investment of capital would cover only the overt types of financial transaction). With these loopholes closed, there can be no doubt that Noel Baker's formula would prove workable and quite effective.

"So far, so good," one can hear the arms merchants saying. "But up to now you've only touched the fringe of the problem. You cannot just ignore the tremendous advantages which private enterprise has over State monopoly—the stimulus which the profit motive brings to inventiveness and progress in design; the salutary effect of competition on selling prices; the existence of an immense manufacturing capacity which can be rapidly expanded in the change-over from peace- to war-time production; the economic value of the peace-time export trade in arms. The sacrifice of these very real advantages would be a heavy price to pay for the uncertain benefits of nationalization."

". . . *these very real advantages.*" *Are* they so very real? Are they, in fact, the exclusive attributes of private enterprise, and would they be sacrificed were the arms industry to be nationalized? We shall find that the abolition of private manufacture would, as far as these factors are concerned, be less grievous a sacrifice than the arms merchants and their apologists would have us believe. But before examining the claims put forward by the private armament interests, let us be quite certain that inventiveness and improvement of design are, *in all circumstances*, things to be desired.

The most efficient, death-dealing instrument used by the
British Army in the last war was the Lewis machine-gun. It
was a weighty, rather clumsy instrument, needing a normal
crew of two. Its production was costly both in man-hours and
material, and there was thus a limit to the number of these
guns which might be employed on any particular section of the
front. Their daily, chattering toll of human life was, however,
prodigious.

The modern army has outgrown the Lewis gun. It has
been succeeded by the Thompson and Sten sub-machine guns—
light, portable instruments with greater firing-powers and capable
of mass-production on almost the scale of the ordinary rifle.
Twenty-five years ago, only a few soldiers in every battalion had
the means of dealing out death on a really grand scale. *Today,
every single man in an assault company can be equipped to blot out lives
at the rate of dozens a minute.*[1]

Then consider the bomber. At the beginning of the last war,
the bomber was a slow, single-engined biplane with a crew of one
or two. Over the target, the pilot had to lift the light bomb up
from the floor of the cockpit and drop it over the side. It could be
a source of some embarrassment to the people below, but destruction was on a limited scale. The salient features of the
modern bomber are only too familiar to civilians and Servicemen
in this war. One squadron of these sinister aerial giants can be
loaded with sufficient high-explosive material to reduce a fair-
sized town to a waste of smouldering ruins and twisted, tortured
bodies.

Here are two simple examples of the "benefits" to be derived
from inventiveness and progress in design. And, considering the
truly amazing "improvements" which a hundred years have
effected in death-dealing instruments, there is no logical reason

---

[1] And science marches on. . . . *The American Exporter* of August 6, 1943,
contained a full-page advertisement which described, among similar items, the
"H. & R. sub-machine gun".

"Six and a half pounds of controlled dynamite. Cyclic rate about eight
shots per second and man-killing accuracy at 300 yards."

Readers were invited to write for a manual illustrating "this great gun . . . . a
fascinating study for every gun fan". The advertisement appeared under the
general heading: "*Great Post-War Line*".

why the next hundred years should not produce an instrument for reducing the world's population by a half in the space of a few hours. Obviously, in the absence of an internationally-organized peace, every nation is driven, willy-nilly, to develop or acquire new processes and inventions against the ever-present threat of war.

But, *assuming for the moment that inventiveness in the matter of armaments is a good thing*, let us examine the manufacturers' claim that private enterprise—and not nationalization—produces the best results. The manufacturers assert that it is the material reward held out by private enterprise that stimulates all that is best in the field of research and invention; that if it were not for the existence of keen, aggressive competition as between one manufacturer and another all technical progress would be slow, cautious and uneventful; that scientists and technicians who are full-time, salaried employees of the State must always lack the incentive that drives their fellows in private industry to seek fame and fortune.

A few examples, chosen at random from a mass of evidence, will suffice to expose the falseness of this argument. Thompson, the inventor of the machine-gun referred to above, conceived, developed and perfected his idea while he was Assistant Chief of Ordnance in the United States Army. *He then resigned and set up a private business to exploit the weapon on a commercial scale—to the greater glory of the Chicago gangsters and Hitler's S.S.* The Lewis gun was invented and developed by Col. I. N. Lewis, also of the U.S. Army, and it was an employee of the U.S. Government who developed and perfected the instruments used in blind flying. The four inventors of the terrible RDX, an explosive more devastating than any the world has ever known, were all scientists in the employment of the British Government, and the man who developed the jet-propelled airplane for the R.A.F. was a professional Air Force officer. With the exception of Thompson, all the men mentioned above produced their inventions in the ordinary line of duty, *and with no intention of deriving personal gain from their exploitation by profit-making organizations.* The reader will have his own opinion as to the ultimate value of their work;

but it is obvious that the profit-motive was the least important of the various incentives at play.

It would be dishonest to pretend that, in a capitalist society, the stimulus of private gain does not act as a powerful incentive to inventors, but since we are judging the whole question in the light of the national interest and of differential military advantage against foreign nations, we must introduce one decisive advantage which Government monopoly has over private enterprise. *When the State gets hold of a military invention it can, if it wishes, keep it to itself—for obvious reasons. For reasons which are equally obvious, the private manufacturer sells it to as many countries, apart from his own, as are willing to buy it at the price he demands.* The instances in which nationals of a particular country have sold inventions of first-rate military importance to potential enemies are too numerous to list here. One outstanding example was the new armour-piercing shell invented by Hadfields in 1934—a shell which, in the words of the company's advertisements, had "solved the problem of oblique attack at modern battle ranges". At the annual meeting of shareholders in that year, Sir Robert Hadfield declared that "this new shell undoubtedly represents the most efficient shell in the world. . . . This improvement has now removed the last outstanding difficulty in the attack of armour under modern conditions." As Mr. Noel Baker said in his evidence before the Royal Commission: ". . . If ever there was a case in which it would have been in the interests of the British Government to keep an invention to itself, there was a case. . . . In fact, Sir Robert Hadfield's firm, pursuing its perfectly legitimate interests in present conditions, *patented that shell in eight different countries.*"[1]

It remains to examine the arguments that private competition in the armament industry keeps selling prices at a low level (with resultant economies to the State); that, as soon as war threatens, the nation is able to take immediate advantage of an already existing manufacturing capacity in private hands;

[1] After referring to the prospects of increased business arising from the patenting of this shell, Sir Robert Hadfield went on: "We are indeed devoutly thankful for present mercies, but, may I add, for what we are about to receive may the Lord make us truly thankful."

and that the peace-time export trade in armaments brings valuable addition to our foreign exchange resources.

In no other section of industry is the absence of competition so marked as in the manufacture and sale of armaments. In no other section of industry have monopolist combination and "price-rigging" agreements reached such an advanced stage of development.

At home, all the most vital materials in the manufacture of arms and munitions—iron and steel, non-ferrous metals and chemicals—are controlled by water-tight monopolist groups which are able to "regulate" output and "stabilise" prices at whatever level is found to yield them the greatest margins of profit. Abroad, as we have already shown in preceding chapters, the international armament cartels have evolved over the years the most thorough-going arrangements for the division of world markets and the sharing of profits. Private *combination*, not private competition, is the outstanding feature of the Bloody International.

That monopoly-capitalism can sell armaments to the State more cheaply than the State could manufacture the same armaments itself is demonstrably untrue. We have not yet had an official inquiry into the relative charges for armaments made by private concerns and Government-owned factories during this war; but some idea of the discrepancy can be gained from past inquiries made in Britain and America. Thus, it was shown in the Murray Report of 1907 that the average prices charged for rifles during the period 1889–1904 by the Royal Ordnance factory at Enfield and by the B.S.A. Co. were as follows:—

Enfield	B.S.A.
£3 3s. 2d.	£4 3s. 9d.

Similar figures for other articles were:

Sword bayonets.

Enfield	Private firms
7s. 11d.	11s. 5¾d.

Cavalry swords.

Enfield	Private firms
19s. 8¾d.	£1 2s. 9¾d.

In 1907, Dr. Gilbert Slater, acting on behalf of the Woolwich Joint Conference on Discharges from the Arsenal, published in *The Times* the following table of comparative prices :—

Articles.	Woolwich arsenal.			Private firms,		
	£	s.	d.	£	s.	d.
18-pounder gun carriages	343	14	4½	672	7	0
13-pounder gun carriages	400	3	6	631	19	0
18-pounder limber ,,	99	0	1	197	5	6
13-pounder limber ,,	108	9	2½	182	16	0
18-pounder limber wagons	107	9	7	283	12	1
13-pounder limber ,,	118	5	5	184	0	0
Torpedoes	362	0	0	584	0	0

During the last war, the profiteering of the armament firms was checked in three ways—first, by a system of costings and investigation; second, by the establishment of competing national factories; and third, by the Excess Profits Duty. In a speech which Mr. Lloyd-George delivered in the House of Commons in August, 1919, when surveying the work of the Ministry of Munitions, he revealed that the huge sum of £440,000,000 had been saved by these means. He began by referring to the original "profiteering" price charged by the armament firms for a shell :—

"The 18-pounder, when the Ministry was started, cost 22s. 6d. a shell. A system of costing and investigation was introduced, and national factories were set up which checked the prices, and a shell for which the War Office, at the time the Ministry was formed, paid 22s. 6d. was reduced to 12s. od. When you have 85,000,000 shells, that saved £35,000,000.

"There was a reduction in the price of all other shells, and there was a reduction in the Lewis gun. When we took them in hand they cost £165, *and we reduced them to £35 each. There was a saving of £14,000,000 and, through the costing system, and the checking of the national factories we set up,* before the end of the war there was a saving of £440,000,000."

And in 1936 a U.S. Senate Committee reported that the cost of building cruisers in Government-owned yards was $2,116,304 lower than in private yards in 1927 and $1,843,693 lower in 1929. It also found that in 1933 the Government-yard estimate was $1,122,000 below the lowest private-yard fixed-price bid and $5,351,000 below the highest fixed-price bid. The Government-yard estimates on the cost of building light destroyers averaged $1,240,459 lower than the average bids of the private yards and $943,460 below the lowest private-yard bid on a fixed-price basis.[1] In a memorandum of evidence presented by the United States War Department on December 21, 1934, to the Nye Committee, it was stated that the average costs of Government-manufactured weapons were 11% below those charged by private firms.

The following statement, made by the French Minister of Air on December 14, 1934, is illuminating:—

"In the course of the year 1933, at the instance of the Daladier Government, the French Ministry of Finance . . . sought to discover whether the French Treasury could, without incurring excessive charges, buy up and nationalise the private manufacture of arms. M. Georges Bonnet was Finance Minister, and he reached the conclusion that the acquisition was possible without laying any extra burden at all upon the taxpayer. M. Georges Bonnet contemplated meeting the costs of acquisition through the issue of Treasury bonds. . . . *Interest and amortization [provision for repayment] of these bonds would have been largely covered by the economies achieved in the arms market, with the result that without extra expense the State would have become the owner of valuable factories, and thereby brought off an excellent bargain.* That, it is true, is not the main reason for the nationalization of arms manufacture, but it is not irrelevant to emphasise the fact that *the mere financial interest of the State points to nationalization.*"

Perhaps the most perennial of all the arguments put forward by those who favour the system of private manufacture is that which relates to the expansion of armament production in time of war. In simple terms, this argument runs as follows: By far the greater part of productive capacity rests, in normal times, under private control. When the nation faces the threat of war,

---

[1] Senate Report No. 944, Part 7, p. 8.

it is this reserve plant and these reserve facilities that form the real basis for the necessary expansion, of production—not the State-owned ordnance plant. The existence of private manufacture thus constitutes a permanent, reliable and gratuitous prop to the national defence structure.

Now, all this is perfectly true; but it is not an argument against nationalization. If Britain decided to nationalize the armament industry it would simply mean that all the plant and equipment existing in the country at a given time would be transferred from private to public ownership under measures on the lines of those put forward by Noel Baker. *Productive capacity and productive potential would not be lessened; they would merely be collectivized and concentrated under State control.* And it would make very little financial difference if reserve productive capacity were held in Government arsenals instead of by private firms, for when it is held by private firms the Government has always had to pay for its maintenance in the prices charged by these firms and by direct or disguised subsidies of various kinds. Noel Baker has shown[1] that the problem as to whether or not the possession of a private armament industry will increase the power to *expand* armament production in time of need reduces itself to three simple questions:—

(*a*) Will a Government arsenal, with a given amount of plant, specialized machinery, special labour and special managerial skill, expand less rapidly than a private armament factory with the same amount of plant, specialized machinery, etc.?

(*b*) Is a private firm better adapted than a Government arsenal for mobilizing and bringing into production the general engineering resources of the country? Is it better equipped for instructing the ordinary non-armament firms how to carry out the manufacturing processes required; for furnishing them with the drawings, jigs, gauges, etc., which they will need; and for distributing, co-ordinating and assembling the many various products of their work?

[1] Royal Commission Minutes of Evidence, Part 10, p. 282.

(c) Is a private firm better adapted than Government Departments for building the new factories and installing the new plant required to produce those kinds of war material for the production of which all the existing Government and private manufacturing resources of the country are inadequate?

In the light of present-day experience, these questions are purely rhetorical, and we will not insult the reader's intelligence by commenting further on them.

Finally, let us dispose of the quite erroneous argument that the elimination of private manufacture would lose us a valuable part of our export trade. A study of the Board of Trade's statistical returns for any inter-war year will show that the mischief done by the export of arms is—as far as this country is concerned—quite out of proportion to the addition which it brings to our total foreign exchange resources. Over the "normal" period 1924–1933, for example, the total average value of armament exports per annum was £6,000,000, including exports of civil aircraft. When it is realized that this sum represented only about $1\frac{1}{2}\%$ of the value of manufactured exports in general, it will be seen that Britain's position in world trade would hardly be undermined by abstention from the Bloody Traffic. Those who believe that the British Government would be serving the best interests of humanity by placing a complete ban on the export of arms in any shape or form will not be dismayed at the prospect of losing such a fraction of export trade. It would be a poor commentary on our manufacturing skill if we could not offset this loss by producing and exporting a slightly larger volume of goods for pacific purposes. But if the State *were* to reserve to itself the right to export arms from its own arsenals to Dominion and foreign Governments there is certainly very little foundation for believing that overseas buyers would withhold orders. Indeed, it can be argued that such customers would prefer to deal with the agents of a non-profit-making public body than with the agents of the private companies.

Before we leave the subject of nationalization it would be as well to say a few words about the alleged difficulties of defining

armaments and, therefore, the alleged impossibility of nationaliz-
ing armament production in isolation from the rest of industry.
This common objection arises largely from a misconception of the
extent and functions of a National Arms Board.

Such a board would have two main functions. First, it would
supervise the transfer of all specialized machinery; and machine
tools used in the manufacture of armaments from private to public
factories. (It is, of course, to be hoped that when the war is
ended a great amount of 'the equipment now used for war
production can be dismantled and scrapped, or adapted to peace-
time uses.) Secondly, the National Arms Board would be em-
powered to take measures against any firm which continued to
produce armaments or any other material believed to be pre-
destined for use in warfare. A clear and internationally-accepted
definition of armaments is already contained in the International
Convention on the Arms Traffic adopted in Geneva in 1925,
and new additions could easily be made to this list to bring it up
to date with present-day military developments.

We face a slightly more difficult problem when we come to
consider articles such as aero engines and chemical substances
such as chlorine and phosgene which can be used for pacific or
warlike purposes. As far as the home market is concerned, the
Government would, of course, be able to exercise complete
control over the use of such products. But what of the export
trade? How could we ensure that such double-purpose material
was not getting into the hands of foreign militarists?

The best safeguard would lie in complete co-operation between
the National Arms Board and the Department of Overseas
Trade. Suspiciously abnormal exports of products capable of
warlike use would be immediately reflected in this department's
detailed statistics of industrial exports; and, if the exporters
and importers could not furnish satisfactory explanations, all
further exports would be stopped and penalties imposed on the
firms concerned. The position under such an arrangement of a
firm like Vickers, for example, would be quite clear. In the
first place, Vickers would be required to dismantle and surrender
all plant, machine tools, stocks and raw materials which were

incapable of being adapted and used in lawful production. The directors would then be informed that their company would receive no more orders from the Government for armaments or military accessories and that no licences would be granted for the export of such material. Finally, the company would be warned against executing any foreign or domestic orders for products whose ultimate utilization was in doubt. The armament-capitalist will, of course, protest that it would be quite impossible for him to remain in business in the face of such crushing "bureaucratic control". We could surely wish for no more generous tribute to the efficiency of these proposals.

Towards International Supervision

The elimination of the private manufacture of armaments is a thoroughly practicable proposition for any Government that has the strength and the courage to seek the necessary mandate from the people. We believe that the issue has only to be put squarely before the people of Britain, particularly the workers and the Servicemen, to evoke an immediate and overwhelmingly favourable response. But the elimination of the profit-motive from the national manufacture and sale of armaments will not produce an end of the evil of armament rivalry between nations, it will not bring peace, unless it is accompanied by measures for the international supervision of armaments and for the creation of an international authority not only to control armaments production, but to begin the fashioning of the political and economic structure of a World Society. Unless this be done, nations will still compete for the resources of the earth and their nationalized armaments will reflect this competition in the size and ingenuity of their power to destroy.

The one positive international idea which emerged from the last war was the general acceptance of the need for a League of Nations. The League failed because in practice it served as the instrument of the dominant victorious Powers rather than of all nations. The avoidance of a repetition of this mistake is the first condition of success for any new international authority set up after the present war; yet all the signs are that the cause of the earlier failure will be not only repeated but reinforced. Instead of full international co-operation for peace, the conception is gaining ground that the responsibility must rest with the U.S.A., Britain and the U.S.S.R., with perhaps China as a junior partner.

In practice, it is perhaps inevitable that the three Allied Great Powers should dominate the world scene following the defeat of Germany and Japan, but it will be a sad look out for mankind if this immediate domination hardens into a permanent ascendancy.

One could contemplate the prospect wth greater equanimity if the U.S.A., Britain and the U.S.S.R. were approaching the task in an international attitude of mind. The evidence is to the contrary. The progressive disavowal of the Atlantic Charter; Mr. Churchill's ultimatum to mankind, "What we have we hold"; America's drive to grab the oil supplies of the world; and Soviet Russia's insistence on strategic frontiers—these, among other occurrences, make it clear that the methods of nationalist Power Politics are to be maintained. Whilst this attitude remains, it is not likely that the preliminary domination which military victory will give to the Big Three will be surrendered for the equality and co-operation of a World Order under a genuine international authority.

A second cause for scepticism lies in the fact that it is obvious that the three Great Powers themselves are uncertain about their ability to inaugurate a warless world. Whilst disarming Germany and Japan completely, they intend to maintain arms themselves. America announces that it will retain the largest navy on the seas, Britain proposes to continue conscription, and Soviet Russia extends her frontiers on military considerations. Behind the veil of war-time unity one can discern already the preparation for a Third World War.

The third reason for rejecting the view that the U.S.A., Britain, and the Soviet Union can of themselves determine and maintain the conditions of peace is the certainty that their claim to do so would be hotly resented by other nations. France will not be content to fill a subordinate position. Nor, indeed, will Czecho-slovakia, Poland, the Low Countries, the Scandinavian countries.

Nor can any reasonable person visualize Germany, Austria, Italy and Japan, however destructive the defeat of the Axis Powers, occupying a position of vassalage over any considerable period of years; if the attempt is made to keep them in subjection, the tragedy of the rise of Nazism will be repeated in a new form. And what of new Powers? What of India, what of a Federation of Arab States in the Near East, what of some of the South American States? At present the Allied Big Three hold the economic keys (assuming that Germany's industrial plant is to be put in pawn); but with rapidity other parts of the world will become industrialized and the domination of a few Great Powers will be challenged.

Is it not obvious, if the world is to be saved from war by acceptance of the decisions of an international authority, that this authority must be genuinely international, representing all nations, allowing the influence of developing nations to be expressed, welcoming into association nations now "enemies" as soon as Nazism and Fascism have been destroyed in form and spirit, animated by a real spirit of internationalism? No re-shaping of the world by the three victorious Great Powers can be a substitute for this.

A central feature of any international authority would, of course, be a court of arbitration for disputes which arose between nations. There have been such courts for a long period, but they have been ineffective for two reasons. First, because Governments have withheld certain issues, particularly issues of "honour", from the scope of arbitration; clearly if we are to advance towards a World State, Nation States must acknowledge the limitation of sovereignty to the point of accepting arbitration on any dispute which endangers peace. The second reason for the failure of international arbitration has been the absence of any power behind the court to enforce its decisions.

However much we may deplore it, we must face the fact that for a period any international authority which is to exert power must have force available in the background. The real question is whether power is to be exerted by a few dominating nations, or whether it is to be exerted by the genuine international authority for which we have pleaded. The dangers in either case are obvious, particularly the danger that such power will be used, as Allied military force may be used at the end of the war, to suppress social revolutions and national revolts against Empires. But just as national States, growing out of conflicting tribal and feudal loyalties, have evolved their police force, so in the evolution of the World State we must expect to pass through the stage of an international police force before complete disarmament is achieved.

The character and composition of such a force have been defined on many occasions by eminent authorities. It is generally agreed that every nation should make a *pro rata* contribution in men and materials and that recruitment should be voluntary. Nationals of any country against whom military sanctions were applied would be excused service; but the general aim would be to create a force with an internationalist attitude and *esprit de corps*. For a time, no doubt, national armies would continue, but, unless progress stopped, the day would come when national armed forces would be abolished altogether. The one armed force in the world would be the international police force.

Given an all-inclusive international authority, an international court of arbitration, and an international police force, the evils of armaments rivalry could be largely controlled. In the first stages, national armaments would be strictly limited; in the later stages, they would be abolished—the only armament production would be for the international police force. Supervision and inspection by representatives of the international authority would, of course, be necessary. There would be the danger of evasion of international limitations; how far this danger would be real would depend, first, upon the efficiency of the supervision and inspection, and, second, upon the degree to which loyalty to the international authority had been developed among the nations and peoples. World citizenship must eventually become a greater loyalty than national citizenship.

Any effective international authority would require from the first a strong economic department, not only for the purposes of advancing world standards of life, as the I.L.O. set out to do, but of owning and controlling certain international services and co-ordinating the natural resources and industrial and agricultural production of the world in the interests of all peoples.

Aviation, for example, ought to become a world-conducted service; it may be that at first national air services would persist, with the international authority linking up their operations, but as soon as possible the actual ownership and control should pass into international hands, with all aeroplane production devoted to this purpose under equitable national allocation and strict international supervision. This would remove the most deadly potential of armaments from the spheres of both private intrigue and national competition.

As the idea of internationalization became accepted, its scope would extend from transport to essential raw materials such as oil and rubber. This department of the international authority would grow in importance until it became a World Co-operative Board responsible for supervising the production and distribution of the economic resources of the earth to meet the common needs of all peoples.

To sum up: the next steps in overcoming the Merchants of Death are: (1) the nationalization of armaments, (2) the establishment of an international authority with a court of arbitration, and an international police force, (2) supervision and inspection by this authority of arms production in all countries and (4) an international economic board running the world air service and co-ordinating world resources with world needs.

These are the next steps—*unless mankind decides to take a much bigger step*.

CHAPTER IX

FAREWELL TO ARMS

WE HOPE readers of the last chapter have said to themselves repeatedly, "But . . . but . . . but". We hope they have protested, "This is no solution."

We admit the indictment. The nationalization of the armaments industry and its international supervision are no solution. At the best they are only an alleviation, removing some of the ugliest features of the Bloody Traffic, but leaving the fundamental evil of war untouched. In his last moments, it can be no consolation to a wounded soldier, or to a bombed civilian, that he is dying from a nationalized explosive authorized by an international committee rather than from a privately produced explosive licensed by a national government.

Let us, together with our readers, face up to the limitations of our proposals. What would they do and what would they leave undone? They would do the following things:

The moral scandal of private profit-making from the universal sale of the instruments of death would be ended.

Quarrels and conflicts between nations would no longer be incited by vested interests concerned primarily in the dividends of death.

Efforts towards disarmament and peace in the spheres of national and international politics would no longer be sabotaged by Merchants of Death.

The fear that other nations were arming secretly would be largely removed by international control. International arbitration, with an international police force to enforce its decisions, would make recourse to war by nations less likely.

The development of international authority would be an advance towards the establishment of the World State which will finally end national wars.

These would represent considerable advances and are emphatically worth striving for. Nevertheless, the "but . . . but . . . but" persist.

They persist because none of our proposals, nor all of them together, touch the fundamental causes of armament competition and war. The warning memory of the hopes aroused by the League of Nations at the end of the First World War darkens our optimism. Then, elaborate international machinery was constructed, with Geneva achieving something of the reputation of an international capital; but it collapsed like a house of cards because the root causes of conflict and war were not removed. One may build a beautiful superstructure, but, if the foundations are rent by faults and fissures and volcanic eruptions, the house will fall.

If the causes of war remain, armaments will remain. If conflicts deep and continuous remain, they will clothe themselves in antagonistic national policies, in intrigues between groups of nations and other groups, in secret planning for arms production, in illicit withholding of new inventions for heavier destruction. These will persist despite all the nationalization and international supervision that economic and political experts can devise. Behind the scenes, a "black market" organization and an espionage service will be at work, officially disowned in times of peace, but recognized and rewarded as far-seeing patriots when war breaks out.

The authors of this book will fail in their purpose if they arouse indignation against the private arms traffic and leave any reader content with a fragmentary contribution to the solution of the problem of armaments and war. Our hope is that our exposure of the sordid profit-making conspiracy behind the preparations for war may arouse in every reader a determination to follow this subject through to its logical conclusion—the discovery and removal of the cause of modern war and the armaments which are its instrument.

Our study of the more limited subject provides the clue to the solution of the bigger subject. The evils of the arms traffic are due to one thing—the profit-making motive. The profit-making motive, or rather the economic system which incites it, is also the root cause of modern war. Let us trace the process.

Towards the beginning of the last century the industrial

revolution brought in its train the drive towards imperialism. The new mills and factories, with their steam-propelled machines, produced goods with an ease which led to an expansion of economic interest to distant Continents. This happened in three directions. First, the machines devoured raw materials with an appetite which compelled a search in all parts of the world for sources of supply. Secondly, they produced goods so abundantly that the warehouses became stocked to overflowing and new markets had to be sought abroad for their sale. Thirdly, the new ease of production, coupled with the wretched payments made to the workers (often children of tender years), made the owners so rich that their savings became greater than could be invested at home; they sought spheres for investment, often at 20, 30 and 50%, in the developing territories abroad.

It was these economic urges which led to the vast expansion of imperialism in the nineteenth century, reaching a climax in the later years. Between 1870 and 1900, Britain acquired 4,754,000 square miles of territory, mostly in Africa and Asia. The same economic urges led France to acquire 3,583,580 square miles abroad between 1884 and 1900, and Germany, less successful, acquired 1,026,200 square miles.

This competition for Empires, for raw materials, markets, spheres for investment, for *profits,* led to rivalries between the Great Powers, to antagonistic foreign policies, to mounting armaments, to war. This was the scene of universal profit-making in which armament makers were able to conspire in the way we have described in this book.

It is not enough to end profit-making in arms. We must end the competitive profit-making system itself if we are to end war.

We are reaching a stage where this is technically practicable. There is no basic need for competition for the resources of the world. The recent Allied economic conference at Hot Springs, U.S.A., declared, as the Economic and Finance Commission of the League of Nations had declared earlier, that the raw materials and productive capacity of the world are adequate, if fully used and co-ordinated, to meet the needs of all peoples. There is, therefore, no need for the nations to fight for them.

Secondly, economic organization is becoming internationalized. The international cartels which we have described in the armaments industry are paralleled in all the essential industries; they must be transformed into organizations which are not merely international in their operations, but international and democratic in the manner in which they are controlled, removing them from profit-seeking ownership to ownership by the whole people of the world under an international authority and conducted on their behalf by service-inspired administrators.

Thirdly, the world is becoming a small place. Airplanes and wireless have destroyed distance. We can travel from New York to London more rapidly than our forefathers could travel from York to London less than two centuries ago. We can speak to each other all round the globe, we hear of events simultaneously in whichever of the five Continents we live. The possibilities of community of thought, of the essence of world citizenship, and of international political and economic administration are developing about us with breath-taking speed.

But if this World Co-operative State is to be established, the whole economic structure must be changed, and we must begin to change it at home. We cannot end the competitive profit-motived order internationally unless we end it nationally. The centres of imperialism, political and economic, are in London, New York, Berlin, Paris, and the other capitals. It is here that we must overthrow them. We shall require not only international ownership and democratic control of the great cosmopolitan combinations for the service of all peoples; we shall require national ownership and democratic control of the national industries in the service of each people. An international co-operative world will only come on the basis of co-operative nations.

This means Socialism, a socialist economy in each nation and an international socialist economy. It is not the purpose of this book to expound the case for Socialism in detail; we are content to make the challenge, to demand of our readers that they follow up our indictment of one profit-making industry by an examination of the whole profit-making system and a serious consideration of the socialist alternative.

But two things we are compelled to add. The time for this fundamental change is *now*. The war, this terrible disaster to which capitalist imperialism has brought us, has shattered many things in addition to human lives and human happiness. It has shattered nations and ways of living and ways of thought. It has given the opportunity to begin rebuilding from the foundations. We must at all costs use this opportunity to bury the old system, to build the new.

At all costs. This leads to the second thing we must say.

The change from the old system to the new will not come easily, will not come merely because well-disposed people desire it. The vested interests are strongly entrenched even in this world which they have shattered. They are entrenched in all the Governments, with the exception of the Government of the U.S.S.R., and even the Government of the U.S.S.R. has accepted, temporarily at least, the continuance of capitalist power elsewhere in the world. These Governments and the vast armies which they control remain, despite all their democratic claims, the instruments of the profit-making possessing class. They will not allow the socialist change if they can prevent it. The struggle for the new system will require from the people an effort, a determination, and a resolution not less than have been demanded by the war itself.

But there are hopeful signs. Over the greater part of the world opinion is moving radically to the Left. In Europe the Underground Movement, socialist and communist led, will not be content with the return of the old regimes. When Nazism collapses in Germany and Austria, the inevitable tendency will be to make the total revolution to Socialism rather than to revert to the outlived Capitalism of the pre-Hitler period. In Britain the socialist purpose is gaining the allegiance, not only of the working class and of the ranks in the Forces, but of large sections of the middle class, and (with disappointing slowness but with sureness nevertheless) the forces of the Left are preparing for the united challenge. In India and among the colonial peoples the new forces are at work.

The critical moment will come when the Governments of the

old vested interests will attempt to suppress the eruption of the new revolutionary socialist forces on the Continent. Whether they succeed will depend upon the strength and ability of the socialist forces in Europe *and in Britain*.

The margin between the achievement of a socialist Europe and a return to a capitalist Europe may be small. It may turn on our capacity in Britain to prevent the Government from using its military, political and economic power to crush the socialist revolution, upon our power to take the first opportunity to establish a Socialist Government in Britain. A Socialist Britain could save the socialist revolution across the Channel, could co-operate in laying the foundations of a United Socialist States of Europe, could liberate India and the colonial peoples from political and economic imperialism, and could begin the task of establishing an international authority, political and economic, which would be the nucleus of the new World State. We could be confident that the peoples of the U.S.S.R. would co-operate in this task, and it is difficult to believe that it would not inspire a wave of response from the people of the U.S.A.

Whether events during the years immediately before us follow this course or not, the final decision between the old order of private profit-making and the new order of human co-operation cannot be long delayed. It is the fundamental issue for this generation, determining whether the human race shall remain divided in antagonistic national groups, doomed to the Third World War and to repeated and increasingly destructive wars thereafter, or whether it shall go forward to the Co-operative World State where war and poverty will be conquered and the not yet glimpsed possibilities of life in happiness, culture and beauty be realized.

In that World Society the story we have told in this book will be regarded as a record of the behaviour of mankind before it had evolved to the level of human conduct.

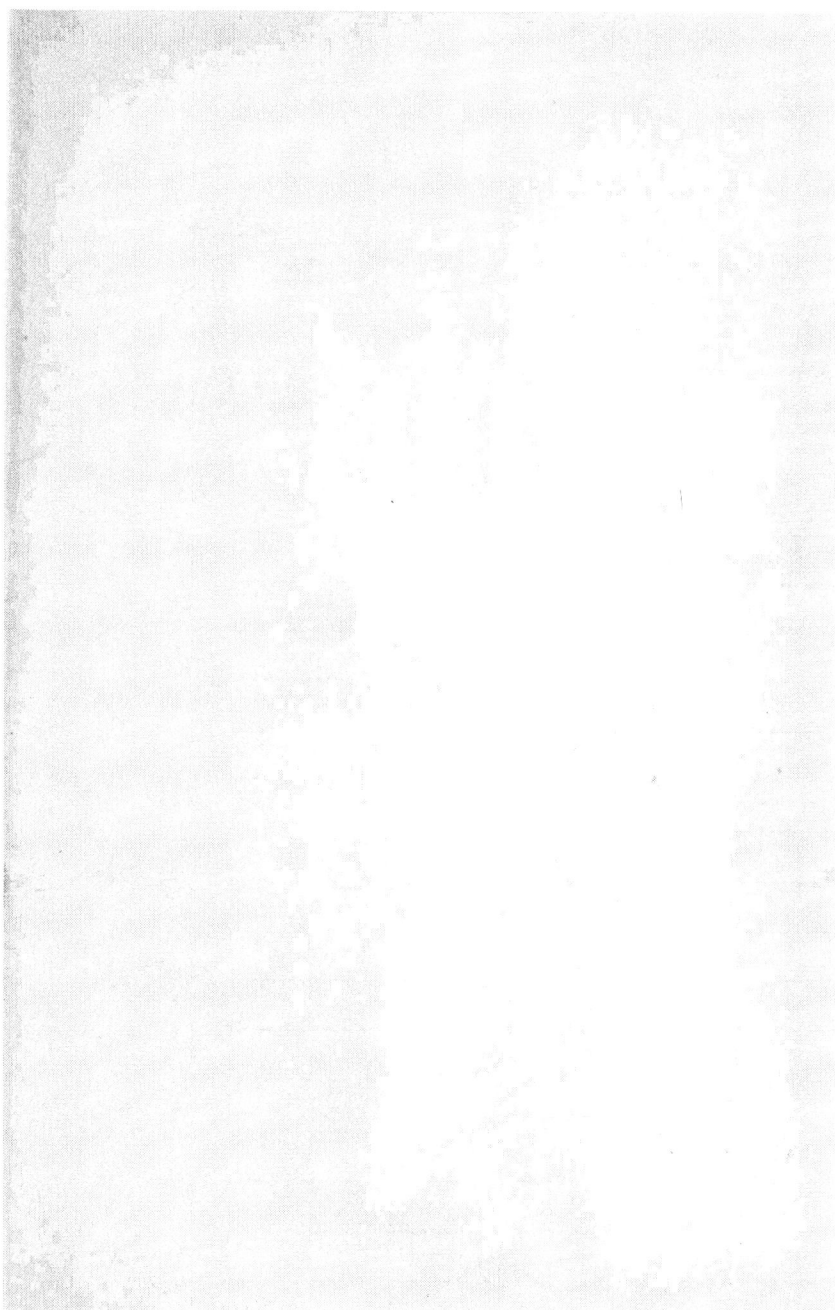

Date Due

CAT. NO. 23 233   PRINTED IN U.S.A.

HD9743 .A2B72 1944
Brockway, Archibald Fenner
Death pays a dividend.

DATE	ISSUED TO
	129480

Brockway.

129480

CPSIA information can be obtained
at www.ICGtesting.com
Printed in the USA
BVHW050457070223
658033BV00004B/17